S0-BBH-357

Praise for Tony Little's
There's Always a Way

"For decades, Tony Little has inspired millions to improve their lives via direct-response television and home shopping. Now, with the inspirational messages and life tips included in *There's Always a Way*, he's doing the same in print. By sharing stories from his life and openly discussing the obstacles he has overcome to create a successful life, this book is Tony's greatest inspirational achievement yet!"

    —Thomas Haire
       Editor-in-Chief, *Response* Magazine

"In four short years, Tony has taken the HoMedics Micropedic pillow to its position of being the #1 pillow sold in the history of the Home Shopping Network. However, his mindset is that he would rather this be considered *significant*, as opposed to *successful*. His *significance*, of course, is that he has positively impacted others with a healthier lifestyle. His significance comes from improving others' lives."

    —Doug Petty
       Director of Sales, HoMedics, Inc.

"I love Tony's style and upbeat approach. His simple steps make things happen. This is a fun must-read for life and business success."

    —Steve DiAntonio
       Chairman and CEO, Color Me Beautiful, Inc.

"Tony Little is the consummate professional for our business. He would be the first person I would go to with a new and innovative product to showcase. I am proud to have been involved with Tony in the beginning of his career and helped start it in some way."

    —George Simone
       President and CEO, Geo Management Corp.

"Tony has climbed to the top of both the fitness world and now the business world, despite numerous obstacles. He has achieved his loftiest goals and now shows you how you can achieve yours as well. If Tony says, 'You can do it!'—you can count on it."

    —John Figarelli
       Executive Director, National Fitness Hall of Fame

"This is an outstanding self-help book—vintage Tony Little. Its title defines its clearly articulated message, and it reads the way Tony sells: with enthusiasm and simplicity, dedication and commitment, humor and energy. Take note of the many parables and vignettes about great poets, statesmen, scientists, artists, and athletes. I believe the message Tony conveys extends beyond salesmanship to provide a philosophy for successful living and a road map for motivation, attitude, and positive self-esteem. An easy read written by an honest, unique, and special person."

    —Herbert Goldstein, PhD, ABPP
       Psychologist, author, and immediate Past-Chair of the Florida Board of Psychology

"Tony Little is one of the most interesting and caring individuals I have ever had the opportunity to know. He is also one of the greatest entrepreneurs and salespeople of this century. This book is a road map for anyone who would like to know how to travel down their own path to success."

  —David Okerlund
   Communications coach, professional speaker, and founder of
   The Creative Communications Institute

"Tony has built a billion-dollar brand. Everything he touches turns to gold! Make that platinum!!"

  —Kevin Harrington
   CEO of TVGoods.com

"You should read this book today—right now! If you have a need to succeed and refuse to lose, Tony shows you 'there's always a way.'"

  —Thom McFadden
   Actor, coach to the stars, and author of *Acting for Real*

THERE'S ALWAYS A WAY

How to Develop a
Positive Mindset and Succeed
in Business and Life

TONY LITTLE
with David L. Carroll

WILEY

John Wiley & Sons, Inc.

Published by John Wiley & Sons, Inc., Hoboken, New Jersey.
Published simultaneously in Canada.

For general information on our other products and services or for technical support, please contact our Customer Care Department within the United States at (800) 762-2974, outside the United States at (317) 572-3993 or fax (317) 572-4002.

Wiley also publishes its books in a variety of electronic formats. Some content that appears in print may not be available in electronic books. For more information about Wiley products, visit our web site at www.wiley.com.

Library of Congress Cataloging-in-Publication Data:

Little, Tony, 1956–
   There's always a way : how to develop a positive mindset and succeed in business and life / by Tony Little with David L. Carroll.
       p. cm.
    ISBN 978-0-470-55841-6 (cloth)
    1. Success in business.   2. Success.   3. Change (Psychology)   I. Carroll, David L.
II. Title.
    HF5386.L73   2010
    650.1–dc22
                                                                   2009041769

Printed in the United States of America.

10 9 8 7 6 5 4 3 2 1

CONTENTS

ACKNOWLEDGMENTS

irst and foremost, I would like to thank my family, my most prized asset in this wonderful, crazy world. Tara and Trent: You have been nothing but the greatest experience of my life. You've stood by me through all my ups and downs, and I'm proud of your good hearts, hard work, and individualism. I love you.

To Melissa, my wife. Your positive attitude, goal setting, and unselfish support of me sitting on the back porch every night working on this book, then coming out every time I needed you to read over some part of it, were really important to me, and contributed to my excitement in writing it.

To my brothers and sisters, who have always been there during my hard times. I don't say it enough times, but I love you. To all members of my staff who make me laugh and who support me with their incredible ability to work hard and smart, and to always be there for me, even though sometimes I am too much of a perfectionist. To Steve, Elliott, and their entire crew from SSA, who, though a big PR company, have always acted more like family toward me. To all my best friends who supported me during the good and bad times, which were many. Thank you—you know who you are, and that I will *always* be there for you. I promise.

To all the people at the different shopping channels and infomercial companies that gave me so many opportunities in the wonderful world of watch and shop. To Kevin Harrington, judge on ABC show *Shark Tank*.

To all the manufacturers and vendors that supported me with hands-on product development and concepts for this book. You are the best of the best.

To the Waxman Literary Agency, especially Holly Root and Scott Waxman, who believed in me enough to represent me. To the prestigious and magnificent John Wiley & Sons publishing company, which is at the highest level of its literary game. Shannon Vargo, Matt Holt, Beth Zipko, Linda Indig and team, who worked hand in hand with me, and who believed in me enough to give me the wonderful opportunity to bring my story to the world. As crazy a story as it is.

To David L. Carroll, who coauthored this book with me, and who has to be the best writer in the world. Without him there would be no book called *There's Always a Way*. Even though there's always a way.

And, of course, to all my customers who have put their trust in me and in my products. And who, by word of mouth, have truly made me who I am today. To all of you, I can never say "thank you" enough. You are positive, courageous people.

Finally, this book is dedicated to my mother, Viola Ruth Little, who was strong enough to change my environment, and this decision changed the course of my life forever.

Best in health and life always, and always believe in yourselves.

Tony Little

ADVERSITIES OF MY LIFE	VICTORIES OF MY LIFE
Almost drowned twice	Didn't drown twice
Shot at twice	Missed twice
Electrocuted twice	Still here today (more creative)
Four car accidents	Survived all of them—barely
My mom divorced	But she helped me grow up sane anyway
My dad kills himself	But found happiness before his medical issues
In trouble with police	Later inducted into the Fitness Hall of Fame
Drugged and kidnapped by predator	Survived unharmed and unmolested
Four herniated discs in back	Won Mr. Florida and Mr. Junior America
One herniated disc in neck	Placed fifth in Mr. America contest
Three surgeries on right knee	Jay Leno refers to me as "America's Personal Trainer"
One surgery on left knee	First celebrity to sell on the Home Shopping Network
Double hernia surgery	My first infomercial sells over seven million videos
Had walking pneumonia twice	Later sold over seven million Gazelle Gliders
Almost died from spinal meningitis	Lived to tell the tale
Very sick from bacterial meningitis	Later made first Gazelle Glider infomercial
Depressed and out of a job	Later won 14 Platinum Video Awards
Still depressed and out of a job	Later won nine Gold Video Awards
Totally broke	Later became Florida Entrepreneur of the Year
Started my own business on a shoestring	Became the most successful TV salesman of all time with three billion dollars in sales
Four reconstructive face surgeries	Published three books on fitness, and still look pretty good
Burned my buttocks in a pool of acid	Became all time record breaking infomercial king
Lived through abusive marriage	Survived abusive marriage
Owed IRS 1.1 million dollars	Paid back every cent in half the allotted time
Forced to auction off my mansion to pay the IRS	Bought a new and better mansion
My son gets hit by a car	My son survives (I love my son)
My daughter has head surgery	My daughter survives (I love my daughter)
I never went to college	Both my kids go to college (almost finished ☺)
One lonely guy for many years	Now married and in love with twins on the way

(P.S. Did I tell you I was held back in first grade? Who gets held back in first grade??? Nothing was ever easy for me!)

But remember: **There is Always a Way!**

Tony Little

1

There's Always a Way to Success

"Life is either a daring adventure—or nothing."

—Helen Keller, deaf and blind writer and lecturer

"I had learned, from years of experience with men, that when a man really **DESIRES** a thing so deeply that he is willing to stake his entire future on a single turn of the wheel in order to get it, he is sure to win."

—Napoleon Hill, motivational business writer

"If you believe you can, you probably can. If you believe you won't, you most assuredly won't. Belief is the ignition switch that gets you off the launching pad."

—Denis Waitley, motivational business writer

"Whenever I hear it can't be done, I know I'm close to success."

—Mary Kay Ash, entrepreneur

There's Always a Way to Success

Always

Always?

Did I say that?

Always a way to success? No matter how hopeless or risky or impossible your situation seems to be?

Well, yeah, from my experience, and from the experiences of tens of thousands of successful people, that's pretty much the way it works. But only if you know how, as *Star Trek*'s Captain Jean-Luc Picard liked to tell his crew, to "make it so."

Hi! I'm Tony Little, that hyper guy you see every time you turn on your TV set—the one with the blond ponytail and baseball cap.

I'm the fellow in the infomercial manically scissoring back and forth on my Gazelle Glider exercise machine and insisting that "You can do iiiiiiiiiiiiiit!"

I'm also the guy who's been bellowing at you on the Home Shopping Network for several decades now, selling everything that's not nailed down, including my own company's line of exercise tapes, fitness items, and wellness products.

Selling is my game—and my passion. I'm confident, enthusiastic, energetic, positive, and successful. I'm always brutally honest with myself and others. I never go backwards; I move straight ahead. After living in this world for 52 years, and after battling my way up from poverty and juvenile delinquency to become *the most successful TV salesman and personal trainer of all time*, experience has shown me one of the few sure things in life: No matter what obstacles you're facing, and no matter what it is you crave the most—financial success, personal success, job success—*there is always a way to achieve it*. That's right, always a way. As long as you're willing to look for it and work for it. As long as you refuse to lose.

In this book I'm going to prove it to you.

I'm going to give you hassle-free, everyday advice that will make everything you touch turn to gold. I want you to be the best business head you can be. And not just business, either. The best you can be, period!

Because everything that applies to selling applies to life as well. If you're an enthusiastic, successful executive or retailer or manager or worker, you'll be an enthusiastic, successful partner, friend, and family member, too. Apply the tricks and tracks of salesmanship I tell you about in this book, and these lessons will flow over into everything you do.

I'll start by telling you my own saga of adversity to victory.

Then I'll tell you stories of both ordinary and famous people who have overcome the most horrendous obstacles in life and gone on to achieve the seemingly impossible.

"A great many years ago I purchased a fine dictionary. The first thing I did with it was to turn to the word 'impossible,' and neatly clip it out of the book. That would not be an unwise thing for you to do."

—*Napoleon Hill, motivational business writer*

This book will motivate you, energize you, and inform you. It's full of commonsense strategies you can use to find your own tailor-made path up the mountain of success to the wealth and well-being you desire and deserve. This book is a no-BS solution to revitalizing your life, and to getting what you want, when you want it. I hope you enjoy it and that you'll pass it along to people you care about when you're finished.

Tah Da, Tah Da!

I once knew a guy who'd just lost an executive position at a big New Jersey pharmaceutical company, and was having a tough time finding a new job. He was so dejected he seemed to have sewn himself into a cocoon and wasn't making any efforts to get out.

I remember exactly the way this poor guy described his brain freeze. "I feel like an itty-bitty little boat stalled in the middle of the ocean," he said. "I'm looking around, but there are no Coast Guard rescue ships steaming in my direction to save me. Where are my friends? Where's anybody to help? I'm in it alone, man, and I'm feeling totally screwed."

Friendless. Alone. Screwed. You feel like quitting. Maybe you've even quit a little bit already? Maybe you've . . .

Yeahhhhhh! Stop right here!

These tough luck stories and a million like them are hard, sure. You're certain there's nothing you can do to pull yourself out of the hole. Doom and gloom.

But wait a sec, my people. *Tah da! Tah da!* Coast Guard ship to the rescue.

"Success is getting up one more time than you fall down."

—*Anonymous*

The fact is, the reality of these tough situations can turn out a whole lot different.

How so?

Because no-win situations and no-exit scenarios, even the worst ones you can imagine—a broken back, a career-ending car accident, a smashed-in face, a drug and alcohol habit (all of which, as you'll see, I've lived through)—can one day turn out to be your million-dollar jackpot in Las Vegas.

I'll tell you why I think this is true.

Because there's always a way.

You may not believe this claim. My advice is to give it a shot. Try living with this thought constantly in your mind: There's always a way. You'll be amazed how a simple phrase can exert so much power for change over so many aspects of your life.

Ways to Success

What are these mysterious ways I'm talking about? Here's a taste:

- You'll find a way to success in life and in business when you start thinking outside the box.
- You'll find a way to success when you change your mindset from negative to positive.
- You'll find a way to success when you get negative people out of your life. Negative people suck!
- You'll find a way to success when you stick to your principles, and do what you know is right.
- You'll find a way to success when you learn to stop saying "I can't" and say "I will."
- You'll find a way to success when you realize that every failure comes with a toolkit for success built in. As famed motivational counselor Denis Waitley puts it, "Failure should be our teacher, not our undertaker."
- You'll find a way to success by setting goals and pursuing them with passion and dedication. "The person who makes a success of living," remarked Hollywood mogul Cecil B. DeMille, "is the one who sees and sets his goal steadily, and aims for it unswervingly."
- You'll find a way to success when you learn to take the initiative, the bold, daring step, in every challenging situation. He who hesitates is not only lost. He's a loser.
- You'll find a way to success in life and in business when you learn to come at the competition with everything you've got, all the time—when you become a lean, mean, single-minded selling machine.
- You'll find a way to success when you learn to sell yourself.

These and many other action formulas are the tools in my own personal success kit. They are the methods that have helped me over the past 23 years to reach 45 million customers in 81 countries, and to sell them more than $3 billion worth of merchandise. They've guided me in my personal life to become a better husband, a more attentive father, a kinder friend. They've brought me health, wealth, recognition, and self-esteem. They're my personal techniques for success, and I'm going to tell you about them in the following pages. They come with my personal guarantee.

Which is this: I promise you right now, with all my heart, that if you use the techniques in this book at the right time, in the right place, in the right way, they will make you a better salesperson *and* a genuinely more effective human being.

Guaranteed.

I Never Saw a Person Go Wrong by Taking the Right Road

Here's a way of looking at life and success that has always motivated me.

Imagine you're standing at the foot of a 20,000-foot-high mountain, looking up. You're determined to climb this mountain and to plant your banner of success at the summit.

But the mountain is very high and very steep. From your vantage point below you see a number of trails winding their way to the top. Some follow a steep ascent straight up. Some zigzag along the sides of the mountain. Some disappear into the woods and reemerge thousands of feet above.

These trails, symbolically speaking, each represent a different pathway—a different *way*—to achievement, riches, and happiness. Some of the trails are narrow; some are broad. They all eventually lead to the top. Your job standing here at the foot of the peak is to use your intelligence, skills, and goals—along with the strategies I'll tell you about—to find the path that works most effectively for you on your journey to success. Then, follow it.

And when you're on top, believe me, the view is great! The famous theatrical producer Billy Rose once remarked, "I've been poor and I've been rich. Rich is better."

It's the same for the mountain. I've stood at the bottom of the mountain and I've stood on the top.

The top is better.

"It's Not Your Fault"

Nope, I'm not going to let it go yet.

I'm going to tell it to you again and again, until it percolates into the bottom of your brain, and prepares you to get the *absolute* most out of the techniques featured in this book.

Remember the movie *Good Will Hunting*?

Robin Williams is a psychiatrist, and Matt Damon plays Will Hunting, a troubled young man who also happens to be a world-class genius.

Remember the scene where Williams keeps assuring Damon that the terrible things that have happened to him in his young life are not his fault?

Williams says these words to his young patient quietly at first: "It's not your fault."

Damon nods and smiles.

Williams repeats them.

Damon looks on patiently, assuring Williams that he understands.

But Williams keeps at it. He continues to repeat the phrase "It's not your fault" over and over again, relentlessly, almost fiendishly.

For several minutes Damon listens to this monotonous mantra with passive agreement. Then he starts to get annoyed. Then he gets angry. Then he gets *really* angry.

Finally, he breaks down and begins to sob.

By repeating a truth that the young hero does not consciously know or believe, or even want to believe, and saying it over and over again, the message pile drives its way through his turtle shell of defenses. As a result, young Will Hunting has a breakthrough of self-understanding that changes his life.

So, for the record, let me repeat the lesson that can change *your* life—and that you, I, and all of us should repeat to ourselves a gazillion times a day. If I could shout this advice to you I would. Since I can't, I'll shout it on the page:

THERE'S ALWAYS A WAY!
THERE'S ALWAYS A WAY!
THERE'S ALWAYS A WAY!
THERE'S ALWAYS A WAY!

Recite this phrase 10 times when you get up in the morning, and recite it 20 times before you go to bed at night.

Work with this phrase. Dance with it. Make love to it. It's got magic in it, and music. Keep it running in the back of your mind like a motor at low idle. Remember it when you're facing a challenge—especially when that negative person at the desk or across the counter or over the phone tells you, "No . . . you can't . . . that's impossible . . . you're screwed!"

"Success is getting up one more time than you fall down."

—*Anonymous*

Use it and profit. Because, as you'll see, when you change your mindset you change your life.

There's always a way.

Tony's Takeaways
- A wish changes nothing. A decision changes everything.
- Make a decision. Right or wrong, it's still a decision. It will make things happen.

- Attitude equals altitude.
- The view from the summit is worth the effort.
- Success: It doesn't come easy. The stars you see at the top in different fields from business to showbiz? You may think it came easily for them. But most paid their dues for 10, 20 years before they got there. You just haven't heard their whole story.

2

Why I've Been Such a Failure

"Having been here and lost, to be here and win, I've got to tell you, winning is really a lot better than losing, a lot better."

—Kate Winslet, British actress
(receiving her Oscar on Academy Award night)

"Ultimately, success is not measured by first-place prizes. It's measured by the road you have traveled: how you have dealt with the challenge and the stumbling blocks you've encountered along the way."

—Nicole Haislett, Olympic swimming champion

"There is nothing better than adversity. Every defeat, every heartbreak, every loss, contains its own seed, its own lesson on how to improve your performance the next time."

—Og Mandino, sales guru

"Two men look out the same prison bars.
One sees mud and the other stars."

—Frederick Langbridge, English poet

Why I've Been Such a Failure

Taking a Chance

I'm going to tell you some things that hurt to talk about. Things that are a little embarrassing, even.

About what a loser I've been at certain moments in my life. About the self-defeating things I've done to myself and others. About how low I've sunk, and how desperate I've been. About how many times my back's been pressed tight up against the wall.

This is probably not what you'd expect to hear from a guy who shouts "You can do it!" to so many people—from a man whose life seems to be a public testimonial to making money, developing self-esteem, and charging people up with super-positive energy.

But here it is.

I'm telling you these things not because I want you to feel sorry for me, or because I think I'm worse off than any other guy.

I'm telling you because I believe that each person's life contains valuable lessons in living—and I want to tell you mine. And also because I've learned that it really doesn't matter what the odds against you are when you're trying to succeed. If you have the will and the drive and the hunger, you'll always find a way.

Look, I have weird hair—a long, teased ponytail. I'm just an ordinary guy. I'm short. I'm loud. I'm hyper. I never went to college. I struggle with my weight. I have a bad back. A lot of times I fall flat on my butt. To be brutally honest, there are really only a few qualities that separate me from all those sad-looking men and women sitting over there on the losing team's bench.

What are they? Just these:

- I believe in myself wholeheartedly.
- I believe that hardships, failures, and obstacles are put in our way to make us stronger—and to help us succeed.

- I believe in doing things a little differently than everybody else, and in looking for simple, commonsense solutions hiding in the complexities.
- I believe that in order to fulfill your true destiny you must use every tool and resource at your disposal. If there are none handy, figure out where they're hidden. They are always there. 'Cause there's always a way.
- Finally, I believe that you have to know where you're going in order to get there. Remember the scene in *Alice in Wonderland* when Alice arrives at a crossroads and asks the White Rabbit which road she should take? The Rabbit asks where Alice is going. Alice admits she doesn't know. "Well then," the Rabbit shoots back, "I guess it doesn't make much difference which one you choose!" Moral: Whatever you do, and wherever you're headed, have well-defined goals. Then pursue them with intention, gusto, and hellacious persistence. You can do it!

"Birds make great sky circles of their freedom.
How do they learn it?
They fall, and by falling, they are given wings."

—Rumi, Sufi poet

Bad Me

When I was a young man growing up, I went from failure to failure and flop to flop.

Every new scheme I tried blew up in my face.

Every time I was about to climb out of the black hole, something pulled me down.

I had a tendency to hurt myself physically as well as socially. My body was violently smashed up in four serious auto accidents. I was nearly electrocuted twice, once while playing with a generator in the bathtub, another time when a short from a hot water heater blew me out of the shower and through a glass door. I fell through the ice twice, almost ending up sleeping with the fishes both times. One day at work I unknowingly sat in a puddle of flesh-eating acid. A few hours later I ended up in a pool of my own blood.

I was born in Fremont, Ohio, a small town in the middle of the farm belt. At 11 years old, when a lot of kids were over swimming in Pete's Pond, I was picking cucumbers nine hours a day in the Ohio sun and pulling cables of copper wire out of broken washing machines for resale. This work seemed like torture at the time. Looking back, it gave me a solid work ethic.

No matter how hard I worked, though, it was never enough to satisfy my father.

"A positive person looks at a 'No' as an invitation to negotiate. They know that there are so many nos that have to be collected before they get to their goal. You have to collect your quota of nos before you get to yes."

—*Tony Little*

He was a grim, violent man, a little like Daniel Day-Lewis's character in the film *There Will Be Blood*. He abused everyone in the family, including my mother. I rarely remember him speaking to me the entire time I was growing up. He spent his days and his nights working at a small oil refinery, trying to make it into a successful business. When his venture went belly-up, he took off for parts unknown, leaving our little family without a word and without a dollar. My mother, a high school art teacher, was left alone to support me, my siblings, and our household all by herself. Many years later my dad settled down and found happiness with a new wife and stepdaughter.

Eventually, though, he killed himself.

Even Badder Me

I had attention deficit disorder (ADD) as a child and as a teenager. This made it practically impossible for me to concentrate in class.

By the time I was in ninth grade I could describe every picture hanging on the walls of the principal's office. I was sent there at least once a week for cutting up in class or wising-off with the teacher. Once I got a three-day suspension for strutting down the school corridor wearing a T-shirt with a picture of a rooster on it and a caption beneath that read "Super Cock."

I was shot at in cornfields by farmers. I got into fistfights. I hung with the local juvenile delinquents. (I don't know why, but I always liked these guys better than the honor roll goody-goodies—probably because they taught me how to cut through the BS.)

My best friend growing up was an other-side-of-the-tracks kid we nicknamed "Dog."

One day Dog and I were walking to school. When we reached the front door I stopped, turned to him, and said, "Hey, Dog, I don't feel like going to class today. Let's hitchhike to California!"

Three days later Dog and I were wandering around downtown Tulsa, Oklahoma, without a dime in our pockets and with no place to sleep. I was for pushing on, but Dog wanted to go home. So we went to a local church and talked up the pastor. He called my mom, who was forced to buy us plane tickets home.

When I returned to school that next week with my mother in tow, the principal took her aside, shook his head gravely, tsk-tsked a bunch of times, and announced that I "would never amount to anything in life."

Years later, after I'd become the most successful personal trainer and TV salesman in the world, my mother liked to remind me of the principal's fearful prophesy. "Remember those words," she used to tell me. "They'll keep you humble."

Maybe, though as comedian Bob Hope quipped after receiving a gold medal from President John F. Kennedy, "I feel very humble—but I think I have the strength of character to fight it."

"The greatest discovery of my generation is that a human being can alter his life by altering his attitudes."

—William James, American psychologist and philosopher

Change Your Environment, Change Your Life

When I was in high school I found my real passion in sports.

As a freshman I worked my way up to become the fullback on the football team. Soon I was dreaming of a Big Ten college scholarship. We had a full schedule of games that year—in Ohio people take their football *very* seriously—and in one of them I smashed head-on into a player named Rob Lytle, who would later play pro football for 14 seasons with the Denver Broncos.

In the collision I tore the cartilage in my knee, and surgery followed. From that time on, whenever I tried to run with a football my knee popped out of joint.

No scholarship this time around.

Then one day, when I was 16 years old, my 22-year-old friend Dave stole an olive green Firebird and took me for a joyride. After running the car into a cornfield and doing a lot of stupid things (like driving the car around in the cornstalks doing doughnuts), we got caught by the police and hauled down to the station. I was a minor, and Dave was over 18. I knew he could do six years for car theft if convicted. So I took the rap and said I stole the vehicle.

For hours on end I sat in a jail cell getting interrogated by cops yelling trash in my face, wanting to know why I stole the Firebird, and where I got the false plates for it (Dave had boosted them in a parking lot).

After listening to my clueless answers for a while, my grillers figured out that I was taking a fall and hadn't really done anything wrong.

They switched their tactics and started urging me to rat on Dave.

I kept sticking to my story. I might have been misguided; I don't know. But I believe in loyalty.

Finally, my mother was forced to hire an attorney, and we headed off for a day in juvenile court. During the hearing the judge called me over.

"From what the police tell me, Mr. Little, you obviously didn't steal that car," he said. "I don't know why you're holding out for this friend of yours."

I shrugged.

"Nevertheless," he went on, "you've definitely been hanging out with a bad crowd here in town, and you *definitely* need a change of environment. Don't you think?"

I shrugged again.

"So let's make a deal. I've talked to your mom and your attorney. They've come up with a way to solve this whole mess. Do you want to know what it is?"

Whatever.

"Your mom says she has a brother living in the Tampa Bay area of Florida, and that he'd be willing for you to come down and live with him and his family."

The judge smiled down at me paternally.

"If you pack up now, move south, and don't come back to Ohio for a couple of years, then this whole case will go bye-bye. Nothing will go on your record. It's obvious you didn't steal the car, son. But you *do* need a better place to grow up in."

I was stunned. I kind of stood there with my mouth drooping.

"Of course," the judge went on, "if you decide to stick around and we have to prosecute this in a serious way, there could be complications. I'm not crazy about the idea, but we might eventually have to ship you off to juvy."

Point made. It was an offer I couldn't refuse. Within a week I was headed down to Florida to a new home and a new life in Tampa Bay. My mom had made a tough love decision that changed my environment and my fate forever. And in the end I learned a lesson that I would never forget—change your environment, change your life.

"I am a little deaf, a little blind, a little impotent, and on top of this are two or three abominable infirmities, but nothing destroys my hope."

—Voltaire, French writer

Impossible Possible Goals

My first few months in Florida were a disaster. I went into a super funk. No one in my uncle's house could cheer me up.

I was a teenage kid who'd been torn away from buddies, girlfriends, house, family, everything I'd known and loved all my life. For the first few months I cold-shouldered every boy and girl in my new school, and kept totally to myself. The more I sulked, the worse I felt.

But there's always a way.

I'd busted up my knee pretty bad on the football field back in Ohio, which meant that I couldn't play sports or gym in the new high school. At the same time, I wanted to do something that was seriously physical, and that would make me feel better about myself.

I came up with a scheme. I'd turn my knee injury into an asset. I'd change adversity into victory.

I went to the school phys ed office and asked the coach if I could use the weight room during gym period. Bodybuilding wasn't looked on as a sport in the late 1970s, and the coach was dubious. So I pushed a bit. Maybe I was even selling a bit, cause I'd already learned that no matter how many "no's" someone throws at you, if you keep persisting in a polite but firm way you'll usually get to "yes."

And in fact, eventually he agreed.

Soon I was lifting weights every day, first light barbells, then heavy barbells, then *really* heavy barbells. Before long I was getting seriously muscled up. I lifted weights in school, and when school was over I marched my growing biceps over to the local gym where I worked out till dinner.

Gradually bodybuilding became part of my daily routine, and then part of my life, as essential to me as breathing. I started to *live* for this stuff, as they used to say on the E! Channel. To paraphrase Vince Lombardi, bodybuilding wasn't everything for me; it was the *only* thing. I was spending so much time after school pumping iron at Dick Fudge's Gym on 54th Avenue in St. Petersburg that some of the bodybuilders thought I lived there in the basement.

Don't get me wrong; my obsession wasn't entirely for the love of the sport.

I enjoyed it to the max, but I *needed* it, too. It gave me discipline, regimentation, concentration—three strengths I sorely lacked. It helped me raise my grades in school to B– level, and it calmed down my ADD. It also gave me a new kind of mental focus that carried over into my daily life. Soon I was planning to go into the field of fitness full-time after graduation.

"I used to think anyone doing anything weird was weird. Now I know that it is the people that call others weird that are weird."

—*Paul McCartney, musician*

I was also learning lessons that I'd use later on as a personal trainer and as a salesman—that self-control is better than self-indulgence, that with perseverance anything is possible, and that failure and difficulty can be incentives for improvement as well as obstacles to it. Around this time I came across a statement by Thomas Edison that I started projecting onto the screen of my mind when I was lifting weights. "If we did all the things we were capable of," Edison remarked, "we would literally astound ourselves."

And one more thing.

Bodybuilding showed me how important it is to set a goal in everything you do. Mine at this time was simple.

I wanted to become Mr. America.

Building Bodies and Bodies in Buildings

I graduated from high school, worked at a bunch of jobs here and there, and started dedicating all my free time to gym work. I had a symmetrical build and a boyish look, two qualities that take you a long way with the Muscle Beach fans. Before long a guy named Dick Fudge, owner of the Tampa Bay gym I told you about, cornered me and told me I had the potential to become a full-time bodybuilder, and that if I worked hard at it I might eventually win some money prizes.

But, bodybuilding, I quickly learned, is a surprisingly pricy sport once you're into it, and young kids like myself needed an angel or two to bankroll their activities—training, travel, equipment, show wear, shoes, gym fees, contest fees, and all the rest. I looked around for someone to sponsor me, and eventually found several backers. Then I started training at Fudge's gym with even greater commitment, and soon I entered my first bodybuilding contest in St. Petersburg, where I won first prize.

It was just a local show, true. But shortly after that I won another trophy, Mr. Sun Coasts.

Now I was starting to get sponsorship offers. I was creating a buzz in the Florida muscle world, working out like a freak to develop my physique into a world-class showpiece, and feeling really motivated to take the science of bodybuilding to new levels.

For more than 10 years the field had been utterly dominated by Arnold Schwarzenegger, the greatest muscle man of them all, probably, and certainly the one who put pumping iron on the map. From the time Arnold started weight training at 14, his goal had been to develop the most perfect body the world had ever seen. He was such an intense competitor that he missed his father's funeral because he was training for an important bodybuilding show.

This kind of fanatic dedication rubbed off on everyone involved in the sport in the 1970s and 1980s, and the competition at the meets, even small meets, was a no-holds-barred deal.

To keep up with the pace, I started practicing body sculpting routines for five or six hours a day. If I wasn't working out I was *thinking* about working out. I'd hang around with other bodybuilders, talk shop, read bodybuilding magazines and motivational books, and plan my next show.

It was also around this time that I began to understand a basic principle of success that I use today to motivate my fitness clients: If you're going to do something, *do it with all the strength and commitment you possess.* It doesn't matter whether you're practicing to become Mr. America, selling socks, or baking a pie. The same principle applies to every situation: no excuses, no holding back, no copping out. Just do it and get it right—all the way to the goal.

Several years went by, and I kept building up my trophy portfolio.

Today if you go into my St. Petersburg office you'll see pictures on the walls showing me posing as Mr. St. Petersburg in 1978, Mr. Southern States in 1980, and Mr. Florida in 1981. I was on my way. Pretty young girls now stood outside the gym waiting to get my autograph. An article or two about me appeared in the local papers. I won the Southern United States division, and placed high in the Central U.S. Body Building Championships. I took the Mr. Florida title (I was the youngest man in history to do so at the time). I was becoming a star in the field.

This is all weird when I think about it now, because at the same time I was realizing that the bodybuilding world during this era had a bizarre side to it, and that a lot of honchos running these shows had *very* scary agendas.

One guy, for instance, a big-shot contest judge, was sponsoring several young bodybuilders who, like me, had their eye on a star.

This fellow—I'll call him Hank—asked me over to his house for dinner one day in a really friendly way. We'd had our problems in the past, but suddenly he was Mr. Nice Guy. He wanted to discuss my career, he told me, and maybe help me out on the money side.

It was a tempting request. Hank was a powerhouse in the bodybuilding business, and he could pull a lot of important strings. But the moment he approached me a red alert went off in my gut. I thanked him and told him I was busy.

Over the months Hank continued to invite me over to his house, always, I thought, a little too insistently. Each time the alarm bell went off inside and I said uh-uh!

Years later, long after I was out of bodybuilding and into TV sales, a friend from the old days called me up and told me some mind-blowing news. My old friend Hank, it seems, had been caught with several barrels full of human body parts packed away in the back of his very large and very expensive home. We're talking arms and legs and heads here. Torsos and fingers. Some of these remains may have belonged to young up-and-coming bodybuilders—like myself.

Thank you, God, for gut reactions!

Another time I was at a bodybuilding show in St. Petersburg and went to use the restroom.

I was standing there at the urinal minding my own business, "draining my lizard" (as a Japanese acquaintance of mine likes to describe it), when I felt a slight prick on my rear end (no pun intended).

I turned, and the last thing I saw before everything went black was this nerdy-looking guy standing there holding the long hypodermic needle he'd just used to inject my butt with a knockout drug.

Afterward the police told me that this perv had carried me out of the building, thrown me into the backseat of his car, driven me all around town for hours, and at the last minute chickened out from doing whatever nasty things he had in mind. Instead he dumped me in a ditch along the side of the road, where I woke up 12 hours later feeling very sore but—thank God—not *that* kind of sore.

And one more story, just for the weirdness record.

During the time I was training for the Mr. America contest I began to notice this husky-looking guy with a sharp, tailored beard working out at the gym. Every day it seemed he'd end up exercising a few machines down from mine. Occasionally he'd look in my direction and smile, as if he wanted to start a conversation. Nothing sexual, I thought, just friendly. I'm not much for socializing when I lift, so I didn't pay much attention.

Then one night we crossed paths at a New Year's Eve party and we got into a friendly conversation.

He had come to Tampa a couple of months before, had been work-ing out for years, blah, blah. He told me his name was Jake—nothing else. Later on when I knew him better I asked what his last name was. He said, "I forget."

We got along pretty well and started hanging together. Before long he was stopping by my apartment several nights a week and we'd go out. Sometimes he'd call at 2 AM to ask if I wanted to go looking for girls. He was a strange dude, definitely, but I seemed to attract a lot of weirdos at the time, so I didn't think much about it.

Then one evening I was watching television in my apartment and the phone rang. My buddy John from the gym was on the line. "Tony," he shouted, "you're never going to believe this!"

"What?"

"The sheriff and the FBI are looking for Jake!"

"FBI!"

"Yeah. 'Cause he kills people. For a living. He's a professional hit man!"

I hung up, stunned. Jake had been stopping by my place three of four times a week lately, and there was no reason to think he wouldn't come tonight. Handguns are legal in Florida, so I took my .38 revolver out of a drawer and tucked it under the pillow on my couch. I sat down on top of it and waited.

An hour later, sure enough, there was a knock on the door. Jake walked in, relaxed, easygoing.

"Ready to go out and party?" he asked.

"Listen," I said, trying to keep my cool. "I got to tell you, man, I just got a call from John. The feds and the cops are out looking for you. They said you killed some people."

Instead of freaking out or getting angry, Jake threw back his head and roared with laughter.

"Hey, Tony boy," he finally said. "That's what I've been wanting to *talk* to you about all this time. I just couldn't find the right moment."

"What do you mean?"

"I've been watching you, Tony. I got a hunch you'd be good at doing what I do. I'm looking for a partner, okay? 'Cause there's a lot of work here in the Tampa Bay area right now. The money's great and the people you hit are scumbags, you know, so that's no problem. You interested?"

My jaw dropped so far my tonsils must have popped out.

"No disrespect," I finally said. I could feel the bulge of the .38 under the couch pillow. "But I don't want to kill people. Just not my scene."

"Hey, look," he said. "No problem. I understand. I respect your honesty."

He glanced down at his watch, real casual. "I guess if the feds are on my ass I'd better split. Too bad. I wanted to introduce you to this hot chick I know."

He was totally laid-back about it, cool as a cucumber. We shook hands warmly, he patted my shoulder, and we walked to the door together.

Then he turned.

"You know, Tony," he said, "that piece you got stuck under the pillow there on the couch. If you were my partner I'd show you how to hide a weapon a *helluva* lot better than that."

He smiled, winked, and left the apartment.

I never saw him again.

Creepy, huh? Believe me, it was all part of the crazy scene taking place in the early 1980s on the national bodybuilding circuit for me.

But you know, the people I rubbed elbows with in the bodybuilding world at that time taught me a major lesson for success: Any time you set your mind to conquering a challenge, there will always be devils standing on one side of your path and angels on the other. You've got to make the right decisions.

The angels are rooting for you to come out on top. They're your friends, your allies. They'll help you win. The devils want to take advantage of you, to use you, sometimes even to hurt you.

Both the devils and the angels will be there whenever you try to improve your life and get the job done. Someone will be waiting for you on each side of the road. Understand that. The two always come together. Help and hurt. Good and bad. Yin and yang.

Sometimes the devils come posing as helpmates, like my "friend" Hank. As John Belk, head of Belk department stores, told motivational writer Tony Zeiss, "Whining about your problems to others is a waste of time. Half of them don't care, and the other half are glad you've got them." (There's a word from the German I learned that describes this emotion perfectly: *schadenfreude*—the malicious pleasure people feel at the misfortunes of others.)

So again, let me give you a friendly warning. As soon as you begin to take charge of your life, as soon as you accept the responsibility for your own actions and begin to improve your outlook on life, somebody will *always* come out of the woodwork and try to take you down.

Why? Because it's so much easier to drag others down than it is to lift oneself up. Positivity takes work. Negativity comes easily—no work at all. There's an old Roman saying: "The road down to the underworld is effortless."

So today when I'm working with clients I tell them that if they use their inner radar to sort out the friends from the enemies, and to avoid mistaking one for the other; if they reward their friends and neutralize their enemies; and if they realize that there will always be bad apples in the lot, *but* that there will always be good apples, too, this knowledge will help them steer an even course between the two extremes, and get where they want to go.

There's always a way.

"Life is trying things to see if they work."

—*Ray Bradbury, American writer*

Look Both Ways Before Crossing

After winning several more important bodybuilding titles I was invited to compete at the Junior Mr. America contest. That's one level below Mr. America.

I won in all my classes.

Now I was Junior Mr. America division holder, and a favorite to take the Mr. America title. The year was 1983, and it was six weeks before the show.

I was feeling invincible. The muscle magazines were carrying articles about me every month. Endorsement offers were flowing in. I knew that if I took this all-important title, my future would be sweet. Winning the Mr. America contest would allow me to do all the things I'd dreamed about—endorsements, TV, marketing my own line of vitamins and drink products, and bringing health and fitness to people across America who needed it.

One morning I was driving to the gym for my 9 AM workout. I reached a corner and came to a stop at a light. While I was waiting for it to change I daydreamed away, not noticing much around me, when suddenly I picked up a giant yellow blur in my peripheral vision moving rapidly in my direction.

The next moment the blur plowed into the side of my car.

It was a big yellow school bus full of children, banging me broadside, opening up the driver's side of my auto like a can opener. My vehicle was dragged for 100 yards with me in the driver's seat. I never saw it coming.

Not Too Cool

The first few minutes after the impact I lay in my seat semiconscious, not believing this was really happening to me, checking to see if I could feel my arms and legs.

Then the adrenalin kicked in.

I opened the door and somehow dragged myself over to the school bus to see what damage had been done. I tried to climb the steps but the driver wouldn't open the door. She was freaked out.

I looked through the window. None of the kids were hurt.

Then I collapsed.

The ambulance arrived and rushed me to the hospital. In the ER I underwent several hours of surgery and other emergency procedures. When I regained consciousness the doctors gave me the bad news: two herniated disks in my lower back, a rotator cuff torn at the shoulder, a dislocated knee (the same knee I'd already whacked playing football), a cracked vertebra, and a grizzly bunch of lacerations, bruises, and contusions running all along my body and face. Not too cool if you're trying to win a Mr. America contest.

The driver, they later told me, had run the red light.

She was drunk. With kids on the bus.

"No idea is so outlandish that it should not be considered with a searching, but at the same time steady eye."

—*Sir Winston Churchill, British prime minister*

Last Bows

During the next few weeks I received many hours of physical therapy, and managed to get it together enough to start training again.

I worked out like a crazy man. But in my heart I knew the fine-tuning just wasn't there anymore.

The strength had drained out of my arms. My muscle mass was diminished. My knees were shaky, and I'd lost tone and definition during my stay in the hospital.

The day the Mr. America show arrived I got it together enough to plow through my routine, though during the all-important posing routines I nearly passed out on stage from the pain. Not many of the judges or audience members knew the handicaps I was working with. Those who did stood by watching me like a hawk in case I slipped or collapsed from exertion. At the end of the meet I placed fifth in the standings.

After the show dozens of people came over and told me how amazing it was I'd done so well, and how courageous I'd been. I thanked them all, and then went home and cried my eyes out.

My bodybuilding career was over, and I knew it.

And so, I thought, was my life.

"It is better to have enough ideas for some of them to be wrong, than to be always right by having no ideas at all."

—*Edward de Bono, creative thinking coach*

Been Down So Long It Looks Like Up to Me

I spent the next two years in and out of hospitals undergoing special procedures for my back and neck.

During one of these treatments I received a spinal tap, then was discharged from the hospital too early. The tap hole didn't heal properly and it got infected. I lost my vision, developed a scorching fever, and spent the next several weeks back in the hospital recovering from spinal meningitis. At one point several of the doctors thought I would die.

When I wasn't flat on my back in the intensive care unit or sitting in a waiting room, I was living alone in a one-bedroom condo in downtown St. Petersburg. I couldn't work out or go to the gym. It hurt too much. To ease the pains in my back and neck, doctors prescribed a variety of narcotic meds. Before long I was hooked on painkillers.

I went months at a time without a job. The few jobs I managed to keep went nowhere. Soon I started drinking heavily.

One time I was employed at a dog food factory. I was working on a bench when I noticed that the back of my jeans was wet. I dried myself off and didn't think much about it. That evening I went home, got into bed, and woke up a few hours later covered in blood. Turns out I'd sat in a pool of industrial acid at the dog food plant. After seeping through my pants onto my skin, the acid had burned away large portions of my flesh.

Another time I was helping a girlfriend groom her big Arabian stallion. I got behind him at the wrong angle and he kicked me square in the balls. (The horse, I later found out, loved women but hated guys.) I then spent a week lying on my back from that one, wishing I had found a better method of penis enlargement.

I holed up in my grungy apartment doing nothing. My telephone fell silent. At times I'd stay in bed for the entire day. My friends, my sponsors, and my fans from the glory days all disappeared. Sometimes I'd lock the door, turn off the phone, and scoff down bottle after bottle of beer along with containers of take-out junk—doughnuts, buffalo wings, bad Mexican food. I had no money, no job, no prospects, no future. I spent most of my hours watching TV or just staring out the window.

Meanwhile, from so much out-of-control eating I ballooned up from my lifting weight of 180 pounds to 230 big ones, most of it flab.

If you've ever come across articles about me in magazines or newspapers you've probably seen my famous before-and-after photographs. The "before" pic shows me on the podium at a bodybuilding show exhibiting myself to a cheering crowd. I'm tanned and oiled, my muscles are straining, and there's a merry winner's smile on my face.

The "after" photo is taken a year later. It shows a shirtless sad sack sitting hunched over in his chair. I have a soggy belly, muscleless arms, and tears running down my face. I look like a depressed version of the Pillsbury Dough Boy.

That was my life. The more I sat in front of the TV feeling sorry for myself, the more I dwelled on the dark side. Everything seemed pointless and futile, and I kept asking myself, "Why me? Why me?" I became like the great pessimist who, whenever he smelled flowers, started looking around for the funeral procession. Finally, I began to have thoughts of suicide. *Serious* thoughts.

Then an amazing thing happened.

I started watching Jane Fonda exercise videos.

3

Why I've Been Such a Success

"If you can *dream* it, you can *do* it."

—*Walt Disney, animator*

"The toughest thing about success is that you've got to keep on being a success. Talent is only a starting point in business. You've got to keep working that talent."

—*Irving Berlin, songwriter*

"Luck? I don't know anything about luck. I've never banked on it, and I'm afraid of people who do. Luck to me is something else—hard work—and realizing what is opportunity and what isn't."

—*Lucille Ball, comedienne*

"Definiteness of purpose and the habit of going the *extra* mile constitute a force which staggers the imagination of even the most imaginative of people."

—*Napoleon Hill, motivational business writer*

"The more you sweat, the luckier you get."

—*Ray Kroc, founder of McDonald's*

Why I've Been Such a Success

Luck Is Not So Lucky

As far as I'm concerned, what people call good luck is nothing but a lazy person's estimate of a hardworking person's success.

"Luck," Oprah Winfrey once said, "is what takes place in your life when preparation meets opportunity."

I really love the old saying, "It's hard to recognize good luck. It looks *so* much like something you've earned."

"I'm a great believer in luck," Thomas Jefferson wrote with his tongue in his cheek. "The harder I work, the more I have of it."

People, I don't believe in luck. Never have and never will.

Experience has consistently showed me (and I have a hunch it's showed you, too) that intention, not accident, gets the big things done in life—that choice, not chance, produces success. When you set out to accomplish a goal with strong purpose—what the Buddhists call "unbending intent"—fantastic things happen. All that's needed is to begin. Right now. This very moment.

My autobiography of bad breaks in the previous chapter is thus not a history of bad breaks at all. It's the story of a journey that started with hardships, but that eventually—as I'll explain—blazed the trail to a new and better life. Misfortune shuts old doors but it also opens new doors. In fact, new doors can't open until old ones close. It's part of life's secret mechanics. "You can't steal second base," the saying goes, "if you keep your foot on first." You have to go for it.

So let's forget about luck. Maybe it exists; maybe it doesn't. I don't know. Whichever way, expecting it to knock at the door and solve all your problems is nuts. Right? It's like sitting, doing nothing, waiting to win the lottery.

Take a different approach. Tell yourself that everyone in the world—*everyone*—has opportunities coming their way all the time.

These opportunities are easy to identify. They have a special taste to them, a special light around them. You've had the experience. When they come, seize them with all your might and run with them straight toward the goal. Then let destiny take care of the rest.

"If you don't know where you're going, you'll end up somewhere else."

—*Yogi Berra, Yankee baseball player*

Luck Had Nothing to Do with It

A woman was stranded on the roof of her house during a violent flood. The town rescue squad sent a speedboat to evacuate her. The woman waved it off. "God will save me," she called out to the people in the boat. "I don't need your help."

A second boat was sent, and a third. Each time she refused. Finally the woman was washed into the river and drowned. Before she knew it she was in heaven, standing before God.

"Why didn't you save me?" the woman bitterly complained. "I waited for you to come."

"Ah, but I did try to save you," the Lord retorted. "I sent a speedboat to get you three times. You just didn't recognize the opportunities when they came along!"

Success and failure, hit and flop, are not separate events. They're two halves of the same whole. Failure is not necessarily permanent failure. It can be the birth pangs of a new and better day.

In a classic 1930s Mae West film titled *Night After Night*, a flibbertigibbet little lady gapes at the gaudy display of jewelry decorating Mae's bombshell body. The woman exclaims, "Goodness! What beautiful diamonds!"

Mae smirks back, "Goodness had nothing to do with it!"

Same for getting what you want in life and in business.

Luck has nothing to do with it. Seizing the moment has *everything* to do with it.

"Life can be pulled by goals just as surely as it can be pushed by drives."

—Viktor Frankl, psychologist

What Jane Fonda Didn't Do

Va va voom! For a 40-something she looked totally amazing in those skintight workout togs.

This was the woman who had single-handedly started the home aerobic exercise craze in America. Her long brown hair was flowing free; her legs didn't quit. The gym setting in the background was casual yet classy. The young men and women exercising behind her looked like movie stars themselves. The music was great.

But in the dark living room of my dingy condo, as I watched this exercise diva perform, a little voice was whispering in my ear. Jane Fonda, the voice told me, was holding back.

It was the mid-1980s and high-impact aerobics was the big thing. At the same time, however, doctors' reports were just beginning to expose the low side of high impact.

Workout fans were learning that aerobics could be damaging to the knees, back, and joints. Especially for people over 40. High impact hammered the vertebrae. Over time it could lead to degenerative disk disease and urinary incontinence in women. It could sometimes cause dizziness and ringing in the ears. The list of potential medical dangers grew longer each year. For some people, the high-impact road was clearly a bit too high.

And another thing.

Jane Fonda exuded expertise as she stretched from what seemed like one side of the TV screen to the other. But wow! The more

I watched her, the more I felt she was ignoring something vital for the health of her viewers. For lack of a better word I'll call it *education*.

There was more to getting in shape than calisthenics. As a certified physical fitness specialist I knew that instructions for building physical strength, strong mental attitude, and lifestyle changes are also essential in any exercise regime. If you're selling health—heck, if you're selling *any* product—give your customers knowledge as well as technique.

And so one day as I was watching Jane and her crew stretch it out, I got a great idea. This was the real thing, all right. I felt it in my bones. Genuine opportunity was coming my way—the seed of an idea waiting to be turned into a successful business. It had that special taste to it.

Hey, I thought to myself. Hey!

I can fill that niche.

I can do what Jane's doing, but also what she's *not* doing. I can give people a video package that addresses *all* their workout needs. I can do it!

"Our plans miscarry because we have no aim. When a man does not know what harbor he is making for, no wind is the right wind."

—*Seneca, Roman playwright*

Who Says You Can't?

The next day I got out of bed *early* for the first time in months.

I dressed in my best jacket and tie, ate a good breakfast, and drove to Westinghouse Cable Company, a local TV station whose shows reached a respectable 200,000 homes in the Tampa Bay area. After a bit of finagling with the receptionist, I landed an appointment with the head of local access cable programming, a gentleman named Jack Taylor.

Standing respectfully at Mr. Taylor's desk, I told him that I intended to produce my own exercise show on TV, and that I'd like to air it on his station. My exercise concept offered a new motivational, nonimpact technique, I explained. It shaped and redesigned the body with minimal stress on the joints. My show would offer the first exercise system in the United States to use light hand weights rather than high-impact aerobics. It would be safe on the joints for people from 9 to 95. It would—

"I don't mean to be rude," Mr. Taylor interrupted, "but who, young man, are *you* to tell people about getting in shape?"

I explained that I had won the Mr. Florida and Junior Mr. America contests, and that I had placed fifth in the national Mr. America—even after a terrible car accident.

He looked me up and down, clearly unconvinced. I was more than 50 pounds overweight, and my face was pale from painkillers and toxic food.

"I can show you my clippings," I blurted out.

"Well, you know, Mr. Little," he said, "we don't air shows on this network for free. You have to spend your own money to produce them. That would be around $5,500 for 15 shows. You'll have to hire a crew, rent a video production studio, recruit actors. Can you do all that?"

"No problem," I lied.

I was already learning the important lesson that in business you always say yes first, *then* you figure out how to do it.

"Good," he said. "Then come back when you have something to show me. If your videos are up to standards, we'll give you a time slot. You'll also have to sign a contract."

I signed the contract, promised delivery as soon as possible, and walked out of the office feeling pretty proud of myself for making a deal with a big-shot TV guy.

But the moment I hit the street I freaked! What did I just do? Sign a legal contract? Am I nuts? Where the devil was I going to come up with $5,500? It was hard enough to find $2.50 to buy the hamburgers I was living on at the time.

"A goal is a dream with a deadline."

—*Napoleon Hill, motivational business writer*

Setting Goals

I went back to my apartment and started penning a list of positive things I could do right away to come up with the money. My list included the following action points:

- **Set a goal.** My total purpose in life is to find $5,500. I am setting this goal in stone. I'll look on this goal as a sacred mission. I'll make it my idol. Everything else in my life—women, jobs, friends—now takes second place.
- **Pursue this goal like a maniac.** I'll pursue my goal no matter how many people turn me down. The more I'm rebuffed, the harder I'll fight back. The more people drop me, the higher I'll bounce.
- **Put myself in the buyer's place.** Nobody buys a product. They buy what the product can do for them. They don't buy a mattress. They buy a good night's sleep. So I asked myself: What product is urgently needed *right now* in the Tampa Bay area? What service can I sell that fills an immediate need?
- **Use my personal expertise.** I will raise money using the skills I already possess: fitness, training, gym administration, and a knack for business and promotion. I will resist the temptation to pursue moneymaking opportunities I know nothing about. I will stay with the knowledge, talents, and strengths I already have.
- **No delay.** I'll put my skills to work right away. Now. Not tomorrow. Not five minutes from now. Or three minutes. Now.
- **I'll never, never give up.** I really want to make these shows. I won't take no for an answer. I won't stop until I cross the finish

line a winner. If one of my attempts to find financing fails, I'll try another, and then another, and another, and another. Persistence is the key to all success. I will not give up. I WILL FIND THE MONEY!

Lists are really empowering. They take abstract ideas and organize them for you. They focus your ideas, flesh them out, and make them concrete. They jump-start your thinking and launch your ship. I strongly recommend them.

Now, one of the few jobs I'd had during my down-and-out days after my accident was selling gym memberships for an outfit called American Fitness Centers. Part of this job was to visit health clubs all around the Tampa Bay district.

During these trips I'd noticed something very interesting. The club owners I spoke with all had the same complaint: The areas surrounding their whirlpools, showers, and steam rooms were always wet and smelly. The manager of one club told me that condensation from overhead pipes was waterlogging her carpets. Another complained that stinky sweat accumulated behind the exercise equipment. A third had a leaky hot tub that had to be shut down periodically for sanitation purposes.

Here was that feeling: OPPORTUNITY.

"If the skies fall, one may hope to catch larks."

—*François Rabelais, French Renaissance writer*

I'm Here to Solve Your Problem

I borrowed a few dollars from the last of my friends and from my mom, purchased some chemicals and vacuum equipment, and started a health club cleaning business that I called TNT Cleaning Services. The business specialized in sanitizing wet areas in spas and gyms.

I then started making sales calls at the local health clubs.

Lo and behold, the moment I showed up and informed club managers I was here to solve their wetness problems, they pounced on me like a doctor who'd come to save their dying child. Clearly, I had put my finger on a problem that needed a fix.

By the end of my first day I had sold *more than $60,000 worth of cleaning contracts*. I took the money, hired a film crew and studio, and started production on my 15 exercise shows.

Where Does Success Come From?

I was too overweight to feature myself in the first video, so I hired three good-looking models to serve as demonstrators while I recorded the voice-over. The video aired on the Westinghouse channel. Within a few weeks it had *outsold every show ever offered on the local Westinghouse channel*. After the first 15 episodes were shown, I bought more network time, produced another 15 videos, and put them on. The second round sold even better than the first.

Success breeds success. I cleaned up my diet, started working out regularly, slimmed down to 190 pounds, and then took over as host in all my videos.

Hey, I was a crazy, hyper-caffeinated kid with a ponytail and a goofy baseball cap. It was something entirely new. Nobody had seen anything like it. I yelled at my audience one minute, pampered them the next. I flexed my muscles, made jokes, jumped up and down, and motivated, motivated, motivated! In the process I began to understand the full selling power of energy and of the human personality. All sales are personal sales. All success comes from one source only—*you*.

Pretty soon testimonials started pouring into the Westinghouse studio from customers who praised my low-impact workouts and described how the videos had changed their lives. People were ready for a change of workout. And I was giving it to them.

Why Rejection Is Good

The next step was to expand video production and to sell my exercise videos on a national level.

But how?

I knew nothing about the entertainment industry, and less about marketing a product on national TV. I needed a production company, a crew, good advice from experts, and *lots* of money to grow the business.

I began looking for cash. I knew a bit about the money-raising game by now, and was prepared to hear a lot of "no's" from the wealthy men and women who could make or break my fortunes. Like any salesperson, I steeled myself against rejection. I knew what was coming.

At the same time, I was eager to do what I'd always done: turn conventional sales wisdom on its head.

Rejection is not rejection at all, I kept telling myself. It's the first step toward acceptance. Every hardship is an opportunity, every "no" a "yes" waiting to be liberated. "Your opponent is your helper," I said to myself. "It only takes one person to say yes."

I sat down and made another list. This one included all the reasons why rejection was good. Here's what I came up with:

- **Rejection is good**—Because all the "no's" you hear boost your determination and increase your will to overcome resistance.
- **Rejection is good**—Because it's like working out. The more psychological reps you do, the bigger your psychological biceps become. You're never really a winner until you lose a few times.
- **Rejection is good**—Because it teaches you to take criticism without getting angry or feeling sorry for yourself. This is a big one.
- **Rejection is good**—Because it instills patience and heightens your powers of observation. From experience you learn that "no" does not necessarily mean no. Sometimes it means "I want to know

more about what you're selling." Or: "I'm not interested so far, but I might be if you can convince me further." Or: "Consciously I think I'm not interested, but down deep I'm curious and want to know more." Rejection teaches you to be subtle, to read your customers' reactions, and to analyze their body language. It's great on-the-spot training. You should pay your prospects for rejecting you! Remember, "no" is not always no. A lot of times it's just feedback.

- **Rejection is good**—Because it teaches you persistence. Are you up to this task? Sure. There's always a way around people's doubts. Find it.
- **Rejection is good**—Because it helps you think on your feet. It steams up your mental and creative juices. It tutors you in the arts of persuasion.
- **Rejection is good**—Because it mirrors back the mistakes you make, and shows you how to avoid them next time.
- **Rejection is good**—Because after hearing so many "no's," it's one of life's most gratifying experiences to hear a "yes." It's like the guy hitting himself over the head with a hammer. Someone asks him why he's doing it. "It feels so good when I stop," he replies. Something like that.
- **Rejection is good**—Because it keeps your ego in check. This is another big one. Rejection keeps you humble.

I read this list over several times, put it in my pocket for future reference, then started pounding the pavement looking for sales prospects, following up referrals, making cold calls, and trying to convince the right people that my low-impact weight training was the wave of the exercise future.

And yes, the people I approached did say "no." In droves.

Some laughed in my face. Some listened to me for a few minutes, then announced they had to catch a plane to Indonesia. At least one person told me, "You're out of your f_____g mind."

Why the stone wall?

I was a man, for one. In the mid-1980s almost every workout video produced in this country featured a woman instructor. Jane Fonda and other high-powered female exercise gurus had sewn up the game. Few marketers were willing to take a chance on changing genders.

Plus I was selling weight training, not aerobics. Who'd ever heard of using hand weights to build cardiovascular strength, improve mood, and strengthen respiration? Only hard-pounding aerobics gave you a real workout. Right? (Wrong!)

Finally, I had no money, I had little experience in TV or film, I was a lowly bodybuilder and thus a dumb bunny, and I had zero name recognition.

Not a great resume, huh? But there's always a way.

I continued to canvas the Tampa Bay area trying to raise money. Finally a local attorney named Joel Yanchuck gave me $100,000 to finance a new video, and that really helped. Orders came in here and there for it, but still nothing spectacular. Vendors liked the video, but they didn't want to go out on a limb. Too much competition from the big guys.

I was starting to have doubts.

Then one day I heard about a new merchandising concept on TV.

It was called HSN—the Home Shopping Network.

The Sound of One Door Slamming

I called the HSN office in Clearwater, Florida, and did my spiel over the phone. Low-impact, safe, fun, brand-new concept, catching on all over southern Florida, a natural for TV sales.

No, no, and no.

I kept calling the network, trying to get an executive on the line.

No, no, and no.

After a while the secretaries at HSN would hear my voice on the phone and simply hang up.

The problem was that it was early in the evolution of interactive television. The only things being offered to home-buying audiences were conventional items like jewelry, shoes, and cosmetics. No one had given a thought to selling videotapes on TV, let alone exercise videotapes. That, and the fact that I was a nobody. This was going to be a tough market to crack.

Then a lightbulb went on inside my head.

"A happy person is not a person in a certain set of circumstances, but rather a person with a certain set of attitudes."

—*Hugh Downs, TV journalist*

Always Take Yes for an Answer

Bud Paxson, the owner of the Home Shopping Network, had a son, Tod, who owned a gym in nearby Clearwater. I drove down to Tod's club one day, introduced myself, and reeled off my credentials as a weight lifter, fitness expert, and champion bodybuilder.

Why was I telling him all this? he wanted to know.

"Because," I said, "I've produced an exercise video that will sell like hotcakes on the Home Shopping Network."

He raised an eyebrow.

"I know, I know, nobody's selling videos on TV. But nobody's selling a lot of things on TV they should be selling. The public's always looking for merchandise that's different, sexy, life-changing. Why limit sales to women's jewelry? Why not sell things that help people live longer and look better?"

"What do you want from me exactly?" he asked.

"Set up a 15-minute meeting with your father," I said. "And I'll spend the next few weeks helping you promote your gym."

Tod thought about this for a long moment, then told me to get in my car and follow him.

We drove directly to his father's house, an estate so large and lavish it had been designated as a landmark in southern Florida. We walked into the enormous front hall and there's the Man standing there, looking down at me. He's like six foot six.

"Dad, this is Tony Little," Tod said. "He used to be Mr. Florida and he's helping me promote the gym. He wants to talk to you. Can you give him fifteen minutes?"

"Five," Mr. Paxson replied.

We went into his office and right away I started making my pitch. After half a minute he interrupted me. "So you're the guy who's been pestering my office every day about some exercise video. I've heard about you."

A bad start.

"It's 'cause it's such a great idea, sir," I protested. "It's 'cause—"

"Let me save you the trouble," he broke in. "We've already spent two million dollars making two of our own videos and merchandising them on our channel. We lost our shirt on both."

I asked him what the subjects of the videos were. One was on first aid, the other on self-administering tests for breast cancer.

"Listen," I said. "Your channel sells products based on testimonials from home buyers. Right? So think about it. Who's going to call in and announce on TV that their breast cancer test really worked? It's not something you want to share with the world. And first aid—is it a good or a service that viewers need *right now*? Absolutely not. There's no immediate incentive to order it. It's not a ready benefit."

Mr. Paxson started at me expressionless.

"It isn't sexy, either," I added.

"You have three more minutes."

When All Else Fails, Tell Them a Story

I took out my "before" and "after" photographs. One showed me in my bodybuilding prime, the other all fat and pathetic. The third picture was recent. "These photos tell a story," I said. "A really great human interest story. Like the 'I was a 97-pound weakling' advertisement, or 'They laughed at me when I sat down to play the piano.' Both classic million-dollar moneymakers."

He nodded impatiently.

"And I have a really great story. I was a national favorite to win the Mr. America contest. A few months before the tournament a drunken school bus driver plowed into my car and shattered my neck and spine. I spent months recovering in the hospital. I was in constant pain. I went into a depression, drank too much, got hooked on painkillers, dropped out. It looked like curtains. Then one day I saw the light, pulled myself up by the bootstraps, started my own business, earned money, produced 15 exercise shows, and got them aired on Westinghouse Cable. Sales for these shows broke all the channel's records. I can show you the figures."

Mr. Paxson stood watching me, unmoving.

"It's rags to riches," I continued, practically shouting now, using my full energy, enthusiasm, and will. "The greatest of all American success stories. And listen, Mr. Paxson, it's *story* that drives a sale. Give me a chance to tell mine. I'll make you *a lot* of money."

He smiled for the first time.

"Tell you what, Tony," he said. "You've got my attention. I'll take 400 of your exercise videos. If the first batch sells in four airings, maybe I'll buy a few more. If not, forget about it."

How to Set Records

The next Saturday a presenter named Bobby Ray went on the air, told my story, complete with "before" and "after" photos, and promptly sold 400 copies of my exercise video "Body Cise" in *four minutes.*

It was a network record at the time. The next day Mr. Paxson called me and said he wanted to order 1,000 more videos. The tapes sold out again.

Then he called me a couple of hours later, but now with a considerably different request. "How would you feel about going live on TV for us?" he asked. "Sell your videos yourself? You've got the salesmanship power to do it. I've watched you in action, Tony. Just get up there and tell your story."

Whoa! Where did *this* come from? Suddenly the chance of a lifetime was being handed to me on a platter. Amazing! Unbelievable! Maybe even a little *too* unbelievable. Phyllis Diller, I knew, was slated to start selling products on the Home Shopping Network. But Phyllis Diller was famous. I was a nobody. Who'd listen to me and my sales spiel?

"I'm no celebrity," I blurted out. "Who the heck knows who Tony Little is?"

"Absolutely nobody," Mr. Paxson blurted back. "But what do you care? Just *act* like you're a celebrity! You get on the show and you say, 'Hi everyone, I'm Tony Little! You know me! Everybody on the planet knows me! I'm a household brand, like Coca-Cola. I'm an entertainment superman! I'm an American icon! Keep saying it and pretty soon you *are* one.'"

He chuckled.

"Let your story do the selling for you, Tony. Bodybuilding champion, car accident, depression, a triumphant rise to success. Behave like everyone in the audience has heard your success story a thousand times, but you're telling it to them one more time because they love hearing it so much."

He let all this sink in.

"It's you and Phyllis Diller," he continued. "Making history. You'll be the first celebrities to ever sell live on TV."

Wow! Here was a lesson I would have paid money to learn: To be a success in this world, act like you're a success already.

I thought about Mr. Paxson's proposal for a moment or two and had to smile. That seemingly tragic event? My accident with the school bus? I'd considered it the greatest disaster in my life. Now here it was turning out to be the ticket to the success I'd always yearned for.

After a minute or less I said yes, Mr. Paxson, yes, I'd like to be the host of my own show. Yes, yes, and yesssssssss!

On Thanksgiving Day weekend, the biggest retail weekend of the year, I went on the air pumped and ready.

After five minutes of doing my "Tony war dance," as Mr. Paxson called it, the phone lines started to blow up. The operators couldn't handle the number of orders pouring in. It was 1987, and engineers hadn't yet developed the technology to handle a high-volume commercial telephone response. HSN ended up getting fined by their phone carrier for monopolizing too much phone line activity that day.

I sold over 200,000 copies of the workout video. In the next few years I then went on to sell more merchandise, win more awards, and invent more products for TV sales than any other television salesperson in all recorded history. As of today:

- I've sold over $3 billion worth of my products.
- I've sold my products to over 45 million people.
- I've been seen on TV in 81 countries.
- My Gazelle Glider exercise machine has earned $1 billion in sales. Approximately 2.5 percent of the population of the United States of America now owns a Gazelle.
- I've sold over eight million Target Training exercise videos and seven million Ab Isolators.
- I've sold four million of my Micropedic pillows.
- I'm the world's infomercial record holder, with nine successful infomercials under one celebrity name.
- My *One-on-One Trainer* book is in its third printing.
- I'm the most successful fitness salesman in the United States, Canada, and the United Kingdom.
- I've won 14 Platinum Video Awards and nine Gold Video Awards.
- I was inducted into the Fitness Hall of Fame in 2006.
- I won the Ernst and Young Entrepreneur of the Year Award in 2009.
- I've been on countless TV talk shows, including the *Tonight Show* with Jay Leno, the *Jimmy Kimmel Show*, the *Jon Stewart Show*, the

Maury Povich Show, the *Ricki Lake Show*, the *Joan Rivers Show*, *Singled Out* with Jenny McCarthy, and many more.

- I have appeared on a variety of entertainment shows, including *Mad TV*, *E! Entertainment*, *Talk Soup*, *101 Celebrity Slim Downs*, CBS's *The Closer* with Tom Selleck and Ed Asner, MTV's *My Beach House*, *Lip Service*, *Best Year Ever 2007*, *My Coolest Years*, *USA Up All Night*, *Party of Five*, and lots more.

- I've been featured on a number of TV news shows, including *Fox & Friends*, *World News Tonight*, *ABC News*, *CNN Headline News*, *World News Tonight*, *Hard Copy*, and more.

- Articles about me have appeared in the *Wall Street Journal*, the *New York Times*, the *Los Angeles Times*, the *New York Post*, the *London Times*, the *Boston Globe*, *USA Today*, *People* magazine, and many others.

- I've been the subject of parodies on a number of TV shows, including *South Park*, *Beavis and Butt-Head*, and *Nickelodeon*. Alec Baldwin and Chris Farley played me on *Saturday Night Live*. A Geico commercial featured me as a personality. HBO did a special spoof show titled "Tommy Little." Bruce Springsteen wrote a song that included me in it.

"All the world is full of suffering. It is also full of overcoming."

—*Helen Keller, deaf and blind writer and lecturer*

Onward and Upward

So there you have it, a life so far. The good and the bad, the failures and the successes.

I didn't tell you all my woes in the earlier chapter to make you cry, and I'm not telling you all my triumphs in this chapter to make you jealous. I'm telling you my story simply because I believe it's living proof of the title of this book: *There's Always a Way*.

I'm also telling you all this because I know that if I can do it, *you can do it, too.*

In the chapters that follow I'll tell you the specific principles that have guided my selling life and my personal life—principles that have brought me the fame, fortune, and friendships I've wished for from the time I was a kid. This stuff really works, believe me. It's the real deal. Use it and you'll see.

And remember, time is *not* on your side and never has been since the clock started ticking on the day you were born. So get going now. And no BS—'cause lying is dying.

Always believe in yourself. You can do iiiiiiiiiiiiiit!

In 1983 Apple Computer stocks were selling for around $60 a share. The next year the stock plummeted and lost approximately two-thirds of its value. Someone asked Steve Jobs, CEO of Apple at the time, how it felt to lose a quarter of a billion dollars. "It's very character building" was his reply. Now *that's* seeing your glass half full.

4

Change Your Mindset, Change Your Life

"It's snowing still," said Eeyore gloomily.

"So it is."

"And freezing."

"Is it?"

"Yes," said Eeyore.

"However," he said, brightening up a little, "we haven't had an earthquake lately."

—*A. A. Milne, English children's writer*

"The way in which we think of ourselves has everything to do with the way the world sees us."

—*Arlene Raven, feminist educator*

"You must start with a positive attitude or you will surely end without one."

—*Carrie Latet, poet*

"The greatest revolution of our generation is the discovery that human beings, by changing the inner attitudes of their minds, can change the outer aspect of their lives."

—*William James, American psychologist and philosopher*

Change Your Mindset, Change Your Life

William Had the Words

School was always pretty much a downer for me. I got into trouble showboating in the halls, hassling the teacher, all the stuff I told you about.

At the same time, I did have my academic moments.

One of them took place in 11th-grade English. We were studying Shakespeare's *Hamlet* that term. One day in class a sentence from the play seemed to fly off the page and hit me between the eyes like a guided missile. Even at my young age, this 400-year-old sound bite of wisdom made a powerful impression, and it continues to influence the way I approach business today. In my workout gym at home I've got this sentence tacked up on a corkboard, along with a bunch of other shake-your-booty quotations that I read every morning before going to the office. (And by the way, I strongly recommend that you do the same: make a list of quotes that get you motivated, and stick them up where you can read them. Take it from Tony—a good slogan acts on your brain like a power protein drink all day long.)

Anyway, a single phrase can sum up a 10,000-word book. Right? That's what happened for me that day in class. You may even know the line: "For there is nothing either good or bad but thinking makes it so."

Wow! What a bombshell!

I'm no expert on Shakespeare and no intellectual. But I'd take it to the bank that in a few seriously amazing words the Bard is telling us that *what* we think in life, and the *way* we think about it, is what creates our personal reality—our whole enchilada.

Think worthy thoughts and good things come back at you.

Think dark, quarreling thoughts, and, well, as computer programmers describe it, "garbage in, garbage out." It's like what my mother used to say: "What you think in life is what you get in life."

That's a strong idea, right? A really gonzo big concept. Every day 10,000 to 12,000 thoughts pass through our heads. And every one of them exerts a direct influence on the way we behave.

How much of this mental activity is pessimistic, would you guess?

Probably more than you realize. Psychological studies suggest that approximately 75 percent of the average American's thoughts during any given day are negative. Amazing, huh!

Yet I confront this negativity in people every day.

I'm talking about people I deal with across the table at meetings, lunch with in fancy restaurants, or meet on the road doing TV shows. These people are caught in an undertow of defeatist thinking. They're angry at themselves and angry at others. Most of them don't realize it, but their pissy hostilities are sucking them down and ruining their personal lives as well as their professional ones. Sometimes I feel like taking these people into my office and hollering at them: "Don't you get it?! Don't you see?! Life could be *soooooooooo* different for you! If you'd just *change your mindset*. Do this one thing and you'll change your life—FOREVER!

"One can overcome the forces of negative emotions, like anger and hatred, by cultivating their counter forces, like love and compassion."

—*Dalai Lama, spiritual leader of Buddhist Tibet*

Your Problem Is Always the Same

Most people I work with know I'm a personal trainer, and sometimes they ask for my advice.

These people are hungry for answers. They know something's sabotaging their lives. But what? Nothing seems to work for them. They're not making it in business or at home. People don't seem to like them, or want to cooperate with them. Why? They're having trouble getting their ideas accepted on the job. Why? They feel bored, restless, out of sorts all the time. Why? Things have got to get better, they tell me. But when?

These are all legitimate questions—or so it seems at first.

Because here's the thing. From my experience, no matter what type of personal problems people suffer from, the diagnosis is *always* the same: a negative outlook toward themselves, their lives, and other people. Their own mindsets are holding them back. And a mind is a terrible thing to waste.

What's interesting about these people is that a majority are sabotaging themselves *and don't even know they're doing it*. Their bad vibes have become so habitual they don't see them anymore. The negativity is too close, like their own skin.

I'm reminded of a joke I saw in a magazine a few years ago. A patient is lying on a couch in a psychiatrist's office and her doctor is sitting nearby holding a pencil and pad. The patient is yelling at the doctor with a hateful expression on her face. The caption reads: "I *said*, 'I just can't figure out why people don't like me!' Open your ears and listen, dorko!"

Change your mindset and change your life.

"Whenever a negative thought concerning your personal power comes to mind, deliberately voice a positive thought to cancel it out."

—*Norman Vincent Peale, motivational writer*

Hey, There's a Cassette Recorder Running Inside My Head!

How do negative mindsets get formed?

Think of it this way. In the first few months of life the thinking-reasoning parts of your brain, your frontal lobes, are a virgin mass of unused nerve cells. These cells branch out in a zillion directions, and make a zillion connections. At this early age there's not much thought data running along the wires.

Then you start to grow up. You begin to think and imagine. Your mind begins to open.

To what?

Neg-a-tiv-it-yyyyyy!

Your parents, your school, your friends, your enemies, everyone on the block blitzes you with a barrage of criticism, backbiting, complaints, put-downs, gossip, fears, prejudices, and sarcasm. Bad and rehab are in. Trashy is better than classy. The media is in there, too, stirring the pot with up-to-the-minute servings of crime, scandal, war, end-of-the-world scenarios, and constant, constant, *constant* bad news.

Every time one of these downer influences crosses your brain it leaves a trace.

After a while these pathways become fixed patterns of thought that become permanently grooved along your brain's neural superhighways. The more you think them, the more deeply they're imprinted, like a trail through a grassy field that's been walked on a lot.

I call these patterns "negative mental tape loops," or NMTLs.

The more you play these NMTLs in your head, the more you believe them. Eventually they come to form the core of your personality, and therefore of your self-image and mental posture toward life. Like an evil scientist at a control panel, Dr. Negativity takes over the lab, pulling levers and pushing buttons, commanding you to think the worst of yourself and everyone around you. It's like propaganda: Keep bombarding people with the same messages, and after a while they get hypnotized into agreeing.

NMTLs are a form of self-propaganda. We all live in a state of light self-hypnosis.

"Whenever you are asked if you can do a job, tell 'em, 'Certainly, I can!' Then get busy and find out how to do it."

—*Theodore Roosevelt, American president*

What's Inside Your Head Is Inside Mine, Too

What's recorded on the NMTLs?

The scripts tend to differ from person to person. But there are plenty of tapes that play in *all* our heads. Here are a few I think you'll recognize:

- My boss (or my teacher, father, boyfriend, agent, colleague, friend, etc.) is never satisfied with what I do no matter how hard I try.
- I don't think she (he, they, all of them) likes me. So I don't like her (him, them), either.
- I'm just hardwired to be a loser (a failure, a wannabe, a clown, low man on the company totem pole). There's nothing I can do to change who I am. I'm stuck with myself.
- When I talk at a meeting (at a conference, to my boss or coworkers), I always sound so stupid (inarticulate, superficial, wimpy, uninformed, wrong).
- I'm too shy (sensitive, afraid, uneducated, low-energy) to be a real go-getter in this business. I don't have enough skill (contacts, experience, cleverness, creativity, charisma, training, stuff on the ball) to stand out and become a major player.
- I'm not smart enough (well-read enough, traveled enough, old enough, young enough) to figure these problems out. Everybody else seems to get them right away. I'm just not up to the task, mentally.
- I really hate this woman (man, kid, competitor, colleague, supervisor). She's a total asshole! If they'd just get rid of her, things would run a lot more smoothly around here.
- I'm too fat (thin, short, tall, hairy, ugly, clumsy, flat-chested).
- Life sucks!

The more we play these loops on our mental tape recorder, the more likely we are to fail. We're the prisoners of our own mindsets. Really. Prisoners. I mean that literally, folks, not like some metaphor. They jerk us around mercilessly. They block us from making money, getting hired, getting promoted, being liked, accomplishing our goals, and becoming a star. They ruin our lives. Negative mindsets are THE ENEMY, people, **THE ENEMY**!

So what are you going to do about it?

That Old Mindset Again

When I turned 50 it was the first time I actually started feeling my age. I started thinking that the number of successes I could have in the future were limited. It was like "Time is running out, Tony." But then I changed my mindset to "I'm actually 30." And then I *was* 30. Just like that. My body, my feelings, my spirit all heard what I told them, and acted accordingly. Everything is mindset. If your mindset says you're 50, and you're worried that you don't have enough time left, change your mindset to 30. The fact is, you should have *no* limits in life. The only ones that exist are in your head.

5

Change Your Life, Change Your Mindset

"When you come to a roadblock, take a detour."

—Mary Kay Ash, entrepreneur

"If you don't like something, change it; if you can't change it, change the way you think about it."

—Mary Engelbreit, entrepreneur

"Fear less, hope more; eat less, chew more; whine less, breathe more. Talk less, say more. Love more, and all good things will come to you."

—Swedish proverb

"Once you replace negative thoughts with positive ones, you'll start having positive results."

—Willie Nelson, country and western singer

Change Your Life, Change Your Mindset

Here's Where to Start

I'm going to tell you the most simple and at the same time most profound idea you'll ever hear *in all your life*.

I mean that! In all your life!

Here it is*:* The reason you feel positive or negative at any given moment has *nothing* to do with other people or with what's happening in the world outside your door. It has *everything* to do with how you react to these influences on a mental and emotional level.

Let me introduce you to my colleague, Nina. During the 2009 economic downturn, Nina lost most of the money she'd invested in stocks and in her 401(k) plan. As a result, she was feeling very sorry for herself and really pissed at the world. She'd become impossible to deal with at the studio.

I work with Nina pretty closely. She's middle-aged, smart, pretty, and well-educated, and has lots of good ideas and a fair amount of ambition. She's also sarcastic, backbiting, self-deprecating, at times needlessly bitchy, and worse, a real quitter when things go wrong.

One day we happened to be talking together in the hallway, and out of the blue she asked if I could give her some business advice.

After work we went out for a drink.

"My money is mostly down the tubes," she began after we'd ordered cocktails. "I'm almost broke, Tony. I feel so damned depressed all the time, I'd like to toss in the towel. I'd also like to strangle those bastards in Washington who did this to me! How do I get out of this mess?"

"The first thing you do," I said, "is realize that the whole problem is your fault."

She looked at me blankly, then started to laugh.

"Very funny!"

"No, I mean it, Nina. I'm not making a joke."

"My fault!" she practically screamed. "Are you *crazy*?!"

"I don't mean it's your fault that the stock market tanked. That happened without your help. What *is* your fault is that you're making yourself so angry and depressed over it."

"Give me a break," she said. "I asked for advice, not guilt trips."

"Listen," I retorted. "I'm a mind reader. I'm going to sit here right now and tell you exactly what you've been thinking for the past few months."

"Knock yourself out," she said.

"You're thinking that you're totally ruined. You're thinking that you have no money left for your old age. You're thinking you'll be evicted from your condo because you can't pay the mortgage. You're thinking if you get some terrible disease, your insurance won't cover it. You're thinking that your friends are going to desert you now in your darkest hour. You're thinking that you'll probably end up living on the street."

I looked at her and raised an eyebrow. "Am I a swami or not?"

She half smiled. "It doesn't take a fortune teller to know I'd be thinking stuff like that, Tony. Anybody would in my situation."

"That's where you're wrong, Nina. Not everybody would. *You* would."

"I have worse thoughts than those, too, believe me," she replied, ignoring my last statement.

"Uh-huh. And that's the operative word here: *thoughts*. That's why it's your fault."

"I'm sorry, I'm not tracking with you."

"Let me be simple about it," I said. "You don't know what's going to happen to you in the future. Do you? Maybe bad things. But maybe good things. Maybe the market will drop some more. But maybe it'll go up and you'll get all your money back. Maybe it will keep going up and break all records. You'll get rich. Or you'll meet a rich man of your dreams and forget all about your money troubles. Maybe you'll get a new and terrific job next month. Maybe you'll win the lottery. Who the heck knows? Certainly *you* don't know."

"I still don't get your point."

"Very basic," I said. "The negative scenarios you're torturing your-self with all come from your own assumptions. They don't come from the stock market. They don't come from the people at the office. They're right here, the currents of thoughts inside your skull. These are the things that are making you so unhappy."

I paused for effect.

"And what makes this whole thing *really* nuts," I continued, "is that your fears are *all imaginary*. Not one of them is freaking real! Not one has happened! Chances are none of them will *ever* happen! You're making yourself totally miserable over nonexistent events! You work yourself up and take it out on others!"

"I guess that's true," she said.

"There's a story I heard," I said, "about a famous scientist. Some-one asked him if he believed in ghosts. 'No,' he said, 'but I'm afraid of them.' That's what it's like for you, Nina. You're afraid of things you know aren't real."

"Attitude is a little thing that makes a big difference."

—*Winston Churchill, British prime minister*

I had her interest now.

"It's not quantum physics, okay? Everybody in the world should know that their thoughts determine their fates. They should incor-porate this simple, awesome principle into everything they do. It should be everybody's working MO. But it isn't. That's the reason why everybody's walking around feeling so fed up and frustrated all the time. They're drowning in their own yucky imaginings."

I paused for a beat.

"So here's where you start, Nina. With your own mindset. Change it from negative to positive, and everything will change with it."

She was silent for a long moment, then looked up. "I get you," she said. "Thanks."

Become a Lean, Mean, Self-Observation Machine

You can never change yourself unless you find out what needs to be changed.

Simple idea, huh? Think about it. If you don't know what you're doing wrong, you can't fix it. "Get to clarity," actor Jack Nicholson once remarked in an interview, "before you get to power."

So here's the next step in building a positive mindset: start watching your thoughts. And while you do, note the link between your thoughts and the way they influence your actions.

I remember the first year after my automobile accident I was mired in self-pity, obsessing over my failed bodybuilding career, my disastrous finances, my smashed health. Everybody'd screwed me, I kept moaning to myself (a good NMTL, by the way). Nothing ever works out the way I want it to (another classic). Life sucks (another).

Then one night I had a kind of awakening. I was sitting on my couch feeling miserable as usual, when I saw my face reflected in the mirror across the room. It was all contorted.

I looked down at my hands. They were clenched.

I felt my pulse. It was beating really fast. My stomach was tied in knots. My foot was moving up and down nervously.

Hey, I thought, these bummer thoughts are having a bad effect on *my whole body.*

This got me going. Maybe I should start paying less attention to my woes and more to the way my thoughts are affecting my body-mind.

For the next few weeks I then began to observe the mental material that floated through my head during the day and the way it influenced my behavior.

Wow! What a world of discovery followed. I didn't need to watch TV anymore. The audio and video inside my head were enough to keep me entertained.

I saw anger, frustration, envy, despair. And I saw these negative bugaboos mirrored in the way I acted toward other people and toward myself. The same old dark, mechanical thoughts kept returning again and again, doing their mischief. There really was a tape recorder playing inside my head. My own thought mafia was doing its thing. Listen to it in action:

- I feel so damned rotten all the time!
- My boss singled me out as a troublemaker and I didn't do anything wrong!
- I can't imagine my idea is ever going to work.
- I wish I had Jimmy's brains.
- That sales rep should take a shower once in a while.
- If I have to carry one more box up these stairs I'm going to quit!
- Why didn't I take that job position when I could have?
- Why do I keep messing up!
- God, I'm so fat!

On and on it goes, an uninterrupted stream of self-criticisms, nay-saying, and complaints. This was my typical brain log for a day.

My negative mindset was clearly running my life, and ruining it in the deal. It was time to do something different, time to take *back* my life—which meant time to get my thinking on a more upward and constructive trajectory. I applied myself to this task with all my might. Gradually, day by day, things began to change for the better.

It was also around this time in my life—and I don't think this was coincidence—that I began watching Jane Fonda videos and making plans to go into the exercise business. It all goes together, you see: Right thoughts generate empowering action, which makes more right thoughts, which generates more empowering action.

The world doesn't make you positive or negative. You do! Your thinking makes it so. As Abe Lincoln remarked, "Most folks are about as happy as they make up their minds to be."

Got it?

There's more.

"Every thought is a seed. If you plant crab apples, don't count on harvesting Golden Delicious."

—*Bill Meyer, radio show host*

"You must stick to your convictions, but be ready to abandon your assumptions."

—*Denis Waitley, motivational business writer*

Find Out the Things You Can Change and the Things You Can't

Every August when I was a kid the carnival came to town.

It was a typical rundown traveling troupe with rides, food concessions, pony carts, a dinky house of mirrors, and lots of carnival games.

One game in particular fascinated me. A barker would hold up five small black metal circles in his hand. On the counter in front of him was painted a single large red circle seven or eight inches across.

The barker took the smaller circles and laid them on top of the big red circle. He'd do this maneuver in such a way that the five black circles completely covered the big red circle. Not a sliver of red circle showed through. Easy as pie. You got three tries to cover the circle for 50 cents.

Of course, once you gave him the money and tried it, you realized it was freaking impossible. The barker had probably practiced this trick for decades. He'd learned it from his carnival barker father, who'd learned it from his father. It was the perfect con game: You thought you could never lose, when, in fact, you could never win.

Through the years this trick has stuck in my mind, an object lesson in how, if you want to "think and grow rich," as Napoleon Hill titled his famous book, you have to know what's possible to accomplish and what's not.

Here, for example, is a "can" and "can't" list I put together to help me focus on my reachable goals. I still glance at this list from time to time. It helps me to stay both positive *and* realistic:

CAN'T DO	CAN DO
You can't change other people.	You *can* change yourself.
You can't change your past.	You *can* change your future.
You can't change the world.	You *can* change your outlook toward the world.
You can't stop other people from being negative.	You *can* control your reaction to other people's negativity.
You can't change the way others speak and act toward you.	You *can* change the way you speak and act toward others.
You can't stop things from going wrong.	You *can* stop blaming the world and other people when things do go wrong.
You can't stop making mistakes.	You *can* learn from your mistakes, and stop blaming yourself for making them.
You can't help having negative thoughts.	You *can* be aware of your negative thoughts and transform them to positive ones when they occur.
You can't be perfect.	You *can* be a whole lot better if you think you can.

Look at your situation. See what you can change in yourself, and what you can't.

Then pursue the "cans."

"Success doesn't mean the absence of failures; it means the attainment of ultimate objectives. It means winning the war, not every battle."

—*Edwin C. Bliss, motivational and inspirational writer*

Transform Problems into Solutions (Because There's Always a Solution)

Don't try to make bad thoughts go away. They're usually too persistent and strong to be resisted directly. Instead, rechannel them into positive affirmations and helpful solutions.

A meditation teacher once explained it to me this way: "Think of your mind as a spinning wheel. You can't just suddenly stop the wheel. It's turning too fast. So you gently slow it down until it comes to a stop. Then you give it a spin in the opposite direction."

Pretty straightforward, right?

For example, say you're thinking, "I can't possibly finish this report by five-thirty." Don't keep repeating this can't-do phrase to yourself. It's an NMTL.

Instead, turn it around. Tell yourself, "If I work hard enough, I can easily get this report done on time."

You have a new job as district manager. You're telling yourself that you can't handle all the travel. Your health won't allow it. You don't want to be away from your family or partner that much. You hate motel rooms.

These are tapes in your head. Turn them around.

Travel is great. You'll meet new people. You'll see new cities. You'll eat out at great restaurants. You'll make important business contacts. Maybe you'll get a promotion. "An adventure," English writer G. K. Chesterton wrote, "is an inconvenience rightly considered."

Say you're pouting over a snide remark a colleague just made about one of your sales projections.

Instead of fuming over it, ask yourself if there's any truth to what she said. If there is, consider it a lesson and learn from it. If there isn't, drop it. End of story. The less you feel resentful toward others, the better you'll feel about yourself. It just works this way.

"How difficult it is for a man to cultivate the good in him when he is surrounded by nothing but evil influences."

—*Count Leo Tolstoy, Russian writer*

Transform Criticisms into Compliments

One of the lessons that psychological researchers consider basic to human motivation (and one of the lessons that so many big cheeses in power positions seem dead set against learning) is that people learn better from reward than from punishment.

Words that intimidate, belittle, and browbeat may get their victims to do what they're told. But these scoldings generate resentment and sometimes a desire for revenge. "The enemy's cold heart summons an arrow to it," goes a Zen saying. As a boss, I've done harsh things to others in my office from time to time, and I'm still reaping the bad vibes my actions triggered. It's not so easy to cancel out negativity once you let it out of the box.

So if I'm a boss and want my organization to run smoothly, it's plain good business sense to deliver corrections in supportive ways, and to avoid angry put-downs and confrontations. Whenever I have negative thoughts about employees or coworkers, I try to turn them into firm but respectful ways of showing my reservations.

In his book *Hypnotic Writing*, copywriter and sage Joe Vitale tells how Henry Kissinger once ordered an aide to write up a report. The aide worked hard on the paper, and sent it to Kissinger for inspection. Kissinger sent it back with a note: "You can do better." The aide tried again, and again the report came back with the same note: "You can do better."

This time the aide rolled up his sleeves and went at it hammer and tongs. He rewrote lengthy passages, edited the manuscript a dozen times, added new and interesting facts and figures, and finally sent it back to his boss with a note saying, "Sir, this is the best I can do."

"Fine," Kissinger replied. "In that case, I'll read it."

People write long books on the subject of overcoming depression and doing better in the world. Frankly, I think a lot of this is overkill. All you really need to succeed is a positive mindset. Really, that's all.

The Picture in Your Head Is Worth a Thousand Thoughts

After I'd made my first exercise video I knew that fitness and TV were the direction I wanted to take.

Cool. The problem was I was totally clueless about how the entertainment industry worked, and about how to market my new concepts.

Then a business associate of mine, a man named John Gallagher, tipped me off about an upcoming convention in Las Vegas called the VSDA—the Video Software Dealers Association. All the major studios like Paramount and Warner Brothers would be there, John said, looking to buy new videos. Why not head out there and see if you can break into the industry?

Sounded good to me. I took my videos and my briefcase, and bought a ticket for Vegas. The night before I was due to leave I then sat down and did some serious visualizing.

I pictured myself at the upcoming convention shaking hands, meeting important buyers, talking persuasively about my videos, signing contracts, closing deals, and selling, selling, selling.

On the plane the next day I played these same pictures in my mind.

By the time I got to the convention I was stoked.

In the ballroom of a super-duper Vegas-style mega hotel, over a thousand exhibitors were hawking their videos in booths, kiosks, halls, and hotel rooms. There was plenty of action everywhere you looked. But getting to meet the really important players was tough. One guy working a booth told me he'd let me talk to his boss only if I beat him in an arm-wrestling contest. (I did, and went on to sell his boss my video.)

Now, the whole time I was working the convention I kept running positive visualizations in my head.

I'd run them in the morning, during lunch, while I was on the floor talking to buyers, and at night before I went to sleep. It became clear to me pretty quickly that these visual scenarios were helping sharpen my mental focus and strengthen my sales technique. When I was out on the floor chatting people up and making sales, I was simply doing what I'd already seen in my mind hours before.

A few days later I left the convention with six offers to buy my tape and to license it to a studio for distribution. When I got home I did an interview for local TV. The host said to me, "But Tony, how are you going to make these videos of yours sell? Nobody knows who you are."

"They will very soon," I replied.

How to Do a Power Visualization

Find a time and a place where you can be alone. Keep outside distractions to a minimum. Sit in a comfortable chair with your back straight. Take a few deep breaths.

Let's say your goal today is to become more patient with the very edgy and temperamental Laura, who works downstairs in the accounting department.

Start by forming a mental picture of Laura sitting at her desk. Zero in on the way she's dressed. See the colors in her ensemble. Take a mental snapshot of the decor in the room around her. Observe her posture, her facial expressions, her hand movements. Drink her in.

Now imagine yourself walking up to Laura's desk. You hand her some papers. She smiles at you. You smile back. You make pleasant small talk.

Then she reads the papers, looks up at you, and tells you they're *really* great. An even bigger smile. Hear her say the words in your head: "These figures are *really* great, Tony!"

Continue visualizing this interaction, emphasizing the harmony and affection that flow between the two of you. Smiles, assurances, praises, kind words, thoughtful gestures, energy, enthusiasm—use them all to woo Laura over to your side. Load your visualization with emotion. Remember your first kiss? You still have a picture of it in your mind, right? Why? Because it was such an emotional moment. It's *feeling* that makes mental impressions strong.

After a few days you should notice a subtle change. Your negative feelings for this unpleasant woman will soften. They may even dissolve. When this takes place it means the visualizations have reached your unconscious mind, and that it's responding positively. Keep at it.

Here's another.

Close your eyes and imagine a giant "NO" looming in front of you. The NO is 50 feet high. Gigantic. It's a dingy gray color or a funeral parlor black. The no-man's-land around it is scorched, colorless, ugly.

Now slowly dissolve the giant NO, and replace it with a giant "YES."

The YES is even bigger than the NO. It's a bright, happy yellow color. It shoots out light from all sides like the sun. It's illuminated. So is the landscape around it—lush forests, running rivers, deep blue sky with fleecy white clouds. See the colors. Hear the sounds. Wonderful!

Hold this YES in your mind's eye for several minutes. And believe in yourself.

As you do, feel the subtle changes taking place in your mood and body. Sense how the YES produces a pleasant warmth in your chest. Feel it relaxing you. Watch your breathing. It's slowing down, getting more rhythmic. Though you may not know it, the moment you visualize the YES your blood pressure drops a point or two, and your energy level improves. Literally *billions* of life-sustaining blood cells and antibodies are being released by your immune system. Your whole mind-body system is fortified. Thousands of scientific tests over the years have shown that when your state of mind turns positive your physical well-being improves along with it.

When you're finished—the session can run for three or four minutes—end by reciting positive affirmations about yourself, and about your relationships with other people. For example:

- I like people even when they act unpleasantly toward me. Everybody has their story.
- When people treat me badly, I try hard not to let them throw me off my stride. I try to be a self-power.
- I take great pride in my ability to be patient with difficult people. A patient person can move the world.
- If people criticize me, I listen to what they have to say instead of immediately rejecting it.
- I am a likable, friendly, forward-thinking person. Others view me this way.
- A positive, helpful, loving attitude is good for my health. It makes me strong and smart.

Repeat your favorite visualizations and affirmations at least once a day. Do more if possible, especially if you're working on a specific problem.

Keep at it. Visualization is truly a powerful, effective method of change. See it! Be it!

Practice Positive Self-Talk (Or: I Like Talking to Myself. Sometimes I Even Listen)

I believe it was motivational author Dr. Robert Anthony who first coined the phrase "self-talk."

"Self-talk," Anthony writes in his book, *Total Success* (Berkley, 1973), "is the constant conversation I carry on with myself as I perceive what I think I see and hear. . . . We build and modify our self-image with our self-talk, using words that trigger pictures that evoke a feeling or an emotion. . . . If you choose to make changes in your self-image, you can use self-talk and visualization to create a new picture that will enact the changes you desire."

Talk to yourself. Say nice things, encouraging things, hopeful things. Do it inside your head or aloud if you don't mind getting stares. Make a habit of it. Tell yourself that you can do it. That all challenges are here to be overcome. That there's always a way. When you're down, give yourself pep talks. They really work. When you're up, use affirmative sentiments to keep yourself there.

Remember this very important point: If negative thought loops work so well, positive thought loops can work just as well. Remember, too: You are the most important person you'll ever talk to.

Avoid Magnifying the Negative

Something's wrong. Things are misfiring. The company president is blowing his stack. The sales for the month are anemic. Fifty people were laid off on Tuesday. You received your second warning statement from the boss.

Nasty. But you're okay so far, right? The sun's still in the sky. Things will get better. Maybe you're asking yourself, "Why me?" Hey, why *not* you? "Shit happens," as the saying goes. But promotions and profits happen, too.

A customer service representative who reports only her customers' complaints and who fails to note their compliments is seeing her half-full glass as totally empty. It's a common trap in business—exaggerating the downside and minimizing the up. The antidote: balanced, levelheaded thinking, followed by purposeful, appropriate action.

Here's my take on the thing. In any tough situation you have a choice: Go optimistic or go pessimistic. Neither of these attitudes makes the problem go away. But they sure do affect the way you handle it. Take a tip from General Ulysses S. Grant. One day his Union troops took a terrible beating in the field. That night after the battle the general was sitting under a tree quietly smoking his cigar. One of his staff members came up to him and remarked on the day's slaughter. "Lick 'em tomorrow" was the general's short but incredibly optimistic reply. And in fact, they did.

Think You Can

Remember the famous kids' book *The Little Engine That Could*?

It's about a pint-sized steam locomotive who's bullied by the bigger engines in the train yard, but who ends up pulling a formidably heavy load of toys up the mountain to all the good girls and boys in the valley below. As he chugs up the steep grade the engine keeps telling himself, "I think I can, I think I can, I think I can." And he does.

That engine is a smart dude. He knows that positive affirmations act like rocket fuel on the body and mind. Believing a thing can happen helps *make* it happen. Really. Sounds like a kind of magic, maybe, and I suppose it is. Try it and find out.

Still, in my opinion the Little Engine made one mistake. Instead of saying "I think I can, I think I can," he should have told himself, "I *know* I can, I *know* I can, I *know* I can." These words get the toys to the kids in the valley even faster. Pithy, powerful thought, wouldn't you say?

Replace the Word *Should* with *Will*

Being a perfectionist, and thinking that you and everyone on the planet *should* meet your high standards, is a no-win game. Avoid the conditional *should*. Replace it with the concrete *will* and *can*.

Instead of thinking "I should have sold more product last month," substitute "I will sell more product next month." Instead of thinking "I should have behaved better to the sales team yesterday," think "I will behave better to the sales team next week." Instead of telling your assistant he has to get the contracts to you faster, thank him for working so hard to get them to you as quickly as possible. Instead of saying "I should work out," say "I will work out."

You get the idea.

Negative People Suck!

One of the more popular products I sold in the early days on TV was a T-shirt with the words "Negative People Suck!" running across the front. I also printed little stickers with the same words for pasting on handy surfaces.

This item sold like hotcakes.

Why?

Besides the fact that it's such a gorgeous T-shirt, *ahem*, its message touches a hot button in people's emotions. It reminds people how sick and tired they are of being dicked around by mean, uncooperative jerks. People buy the shirt to go public with their frustration, and to tell the world they're not taking it anymore—that they're not going to let these negative jerks take them down.

Can you blame them?

The possibility of becoming a positive, successful person is nil if you surround yourself with downer people all the time. They suck the liver out of you—that is, the part of you that wants to "live."

Think about the people you know, that you hang out with, that you work with. Who gives you energy? Who drains your energy like a psychic vampire? Who says "no" all the time? Who says "no" at the wrong times? Whose "yes" doesn't really mean yes? Who's lying to you, trying to fool you, trying to use you? Identify the worst offenders and cut them loose. Sometimes you just gotta say bye-bye to useless things in your life and then move on.

Angry, hostile, bothered men and women make us fail. They ruin things. They look for trouble, and when they inevitably find it they tell you proudly, "See, I told you it won't work! I told you it's a dumb idea! I told you life sucks!"

These people subscribe to the philosophy of the German philosopher Arthur Schopenhauer, who once advised everyone he knew to eat a toad the moment they woke up in the morning. This way, explained the great pessimist, we *probably* won't have anything more disgusting happen to us for the rest of the day.

Happy, adjusted, hopeful people are categorically different. They help us succeed. They make us feel good about ourselves. They make us more creative, more intelligent and able. They help us to see that there's always a way. "A pessimist sees the difficulty in every opportunity," said Sir Winston Churchill; "an optimist sees the opportunity in every difficulty."

A friend of mine compares people to the poles on a magnet. One type is positive and attracts. The other type is negative and repels. Which pole would you rather be? Which pole would you rather be around?

Duh!

The Past Is the Only Dead Thing That Smells Sweet

There's a Zen story about two monks, an older and a younger, who set out on a journey. After hours of walking together in silence they arrive at a fast-moving river. A beautiful young girl is standing there by the shore. She hails the monks, tells them her mother is sick, and that she must get home immediately. The problem is she doesn't know how to swim, so she can't cross the river alone. Can they help?

In a flash one of the monks picks up the girl, swims with her across the river, and puts her down on the other side. The two monks then continue their journey.

After many hours walking in silence, the younger monk speaks up. There is anger and frustration in his voice. "You know it is a sin in our order to touch a woman!" he scolds. "Why did you do such a thing?"

"Oh, her," replies the older monk. "I put that young lady down back there by the river. It is *you* who is still carrying her around."

What are you still carrying around on your shoulders? What negative memories, grudges, losses, and "if only" scenarios? The past is the only dead thing that smells sweet. Leave it and move on. Do what the Beatles advise and "let it be." Right now. Go ahead. Truly powerful leaders use their past *only* as a lesson for building a better future.

Think Positive for Your Health's Sake

Thinking in an affirmative way not only improves your attitude; it provides your body with extra energy to make more calls, sell smarter, and get the job done better. Many scientific studies confirm this fact—that optimism strengthens the human immune system, reduces disease-causing inflammation, lowers stress, and improves performance. According to researchers at the Mayo Clinic, positive thinking may well do all the things on this amazing list:

- Increase your life span.
- Lower your depression and distress levels.
- Strengthen your resistance to the common cold.
- Improve your psychological well-being.
- Reduce your risk of death from cardiovascular disease.
- Help you develop better coping skills during times of hardship, pressure, and crisis.
- Make you a better lover (oops, sorry, this one's mine).

Read It! Be It!

I'm talking about mentors. Friends whose opinions you trust. Sympathetic colleagues and coworkers.

Ask them to give you feedback on your attempts to be more positive. Ask them "How am I doing?" like New York Mayor Edward Koch used to do to passersby in Manhattan. Listen to what they tell you. If at least three people whose opinions you value tell you the same thing, it's probably true.

You can also learn a good deal about developing a positive mindset from reading motivational books. The following have helped me enormously in my career, especially the works of Napoleon Hill and Zig Ziglar. Here's a sampling of books and CDs that I recommend. There are lots of others.

Daniel G. Amen, M.D., *Change Your Brain, Change Your Life* (Times Books, 1998).

Jack Canfield, *The Success Principles: How to Get from Where You Are to Where You Want to Be* (HarperCollins, 2005).

Dale Carnegie, *The Power of Positive Thinking* (Prentice-Hall, 1952).

Deepak Chopra, *Magical Mind, Magical Body* (Audio book; Simon & Schuster, 2003).

Tony Robbins, *Get the Edge* (CD; Guthy-Renker, 2000).

Joe Vitale, *The Attractor Factor* (John Wiley & Sons, 2005).

Zig Ziglar, *Ziglar on Selling* (Oliver Nelson, 2003); also: *See You at the Top, Over the Top,* and *Ziglar on Selling.*

Tony's Takeaways

- You're only as lucky as you are persistent, visionary, and hardworking. Bad luck is the thing that cop-outs blame their failures on.
- Good attitudes and bad attitudes are both like germs. They're catching. Pay attention to who you hang out with.
- There are times in life when it's better to lose than to win. One loss today can sometimes get you five wins a year from today.
- Whatever you do is always the result of what you decide to do. You are responsible for your decisions—and your actions.
- It's nothing but a dream until you write it down on a list. Don't just think it; ink it!

6

Beyond Thinking Outside the Box (What Box?)

"In a crowd there are going to be hundreds of thinkers. Among these hundreds there is going to be one out-of-the-box thinker—if you're lucky."

—Ruth Cristello, blogger

"The older I get, the more centered I become and the more I think I really know about myself. What I know is that what other people do doesn't really have any effect on me."

—Oprah Winfrey, talk show host

"Think like a man of action, act like a man of thought."

—Henri Bergson, French philosopher

"Why live out of the box? To live. To be. To create. To renew."

—Mike Vance, motivational speaker

"Chaos often breeds life, when order breeds habit."

—Henry Adams, American writer

Beyond Thinking Outside the Box (What Box?)

Where Were You When 9/11 Took Place?

I remember exactly where.

I was in New York City, in the elevator of the New York Hilton—a couple of miles from Ground Zero.

The TV set was on in the elevator and I was kind of half staring at it when an image flashed on screen. It showed a heartbreaking sight, a commercial jetliner smashing into one of the Twin Towers and bursting into a terrible fireball.

I hurried to my room, turned on the TV, and called my manager, Ray Manzella, who was staying at the Waldorf Astoria Hotel across town. I told him to turn on his set.

That's when the second plane hit.

A newscaster on the TV announced that the Pentagon had been targeted, and that a jetliner headed for the White House had crashed in the middle of Pennsylvania. Had other landmarks in New York City been hit? Were these disasters part of an attack across the United States? Would this tragedy trigger World War III?

My thoughts went directly to my young son and daughter in Tampa. Were they safe? Were they protected? I had to get down there and be with them as soon as possible.

As it happened, I keep a town car in New York for running around the city whenever I'm there, which is a lot. That very minute, the limo was waiting for me downstairs in front of the hotel with my New York driver at the wheel. Still on the phone, I told Ray I'd pick him up as soon as I could, and we'd get out of town pronto.

But when I swung by the Waldorf and Ray jumped into the car, he started begging me to stop at a hotel up the street where his girlfriend was staying. He wanted to take her with us. Ray loves the girls.

I agreed and we drove a few blocks to the hotel. Ray got out and dashed into the lobby.

I then sat there for what seemed like hours, glancing at my watch, trying to reach my kids on the cell phone (it was always busy), and witnessing the mass craziness in the streets outside. There was smoke everywhere. Horns were blasting, cars were peeling out and running red lights, people were wandering around in a daze, fire engines were racing the wrong way down one-way streets, lines of what seemed like hundreds of police cars were driving by with sirens blaring and lights whirling. Over the news I heard that the city was closing all bridges and airports, and that mass transit was being shut down.

I asked my driver if he had any idea what we should do. I told him I wanted to drive to a friend's house in Montclair, a New Jersey suburb across the Hudson. I would regroup there, make some phone calls, eat something, clear my head, take the wheel of my limo, and drive straight down to Tampa.

The driver thought for a moment, then said he knew a route we could take out of the city without crossing any New York City bridges.

I told him we should go for it.

"It is better to have enough ideas for some of them to be wrong, than to be always right by having no ideas at all."

—*Edward de Bono, creative thinking coach*

Think What Others Aren't Thinking

As I was sitting there waiting for Ray to show up, an attractive, expensively dressed middle-aged woman suddenly ran up to my limo and started pounding on the window. Totally weirded out, she was yelling that she had to get to Connecticut where she lived right away, and that she wanted to *buy* my limousine right now, on the spot.

I told her it wasn't for sale.

"Then let me come with you!" she pleaded. "I'll pay whatever you like!"

I told her to jump in and to forget about the money. We'd find a way, I said. (I later discovered she was heiress to a vast canned food fortune and could have bought me *and* my limo a dozen times over.)

A few minutes later Ray came out of the hotel *without* his girlfriend—he never told me why—and we were out of there.

Five hours later, after encountering endless blockades and detours, we reached my friend's home in Montclair. During the trip the rich lady complained continually to everybody—she had to feed her dog, her husband would have a heart attack, the terrorists were invading.

Five hours of this lady's voice was enough for one day. I told my driver to chauffeur her to wherever she wanted to go in Connecticut, then to take the limo and drive himself home. I'd figure out a way to get to Florida on my own. I then borrowed my friend's car, and started making the rounds of auto dealers and rental agencies in the Montclair area.

Wow! Let me tell you, I was not prepared for what happened next.

Not a *single car* was available to rent at any of these agencies. Nada. It turned out that other people had the same idea as me, and had emptied the lots.

What now? I *had* to get home to my kids. I decided to do what I always did in time of crisis. I took a few deep breaths, relaxed, let my mind go blank, and told myself *there's always a way*. I opened my mind to whatever solutions wanted to come in. A few minutes later I was on the road again.

There were no cars to rent anywhere for 50 miles around. This was true.

So—why not rent a *truck*?

I drove over to a Ryder Truck Rentals, and sure enough, they had dozens of shiny new models waiting for me on the lot. In their panic, everyone in northern Jersey was thinking "car." Nobody was thinking "truck."

Twenty minutes later I climbed into the cab of a 22-foot-long yellow big box, fired it up, and drove back to the house to pick up Ray, whose eyes bulged when he saw me pull up in this monster. We then drove for 22 straight hours until we reached my home—and my kids—in Tampa.

"Imagination is more important than knowledge."

—*Albert Einstein, physicist*

Beyond Thinking Outside the Box

Why am I telling you this story?

Because it illustrates a technique I like to use when facing tough situations.

During the crunch times, you have to stretch your inner resources, lift your thinking out of the ordinary, see things in a way that others don't, and do things that others don't do. I never put limits on my capabilities. You shouldn't, either.

I'll give you an example.

In the period of 1980 to 1981 when I was working toward the goal of winning the Mr. America contest, I had several ugly run-ins with the chairman of the Amateur Athletic Union (AAU), a guy who was more or less running things in the bodybuilding world at the time (and who shall remain nameless).

At the Mr. Southern States contest that year I had taken the prize for "best poser," "most muscular," and "most symmetrical." These are your top three awards. But when the time came to choose Best of Show that day, the judges, led by this chairman, gave the trophy to another contestant although *everyone* who was watching agreed I was the winner, hands down.

This opinion was confirmed when the evil chairman came up to me after the show and whispered into my ear: "Listen up, Tony. You're only going to go as far as I *want* you to go in this sport."

It was kind of like telling me I was done in the bodybuilding world forever.

Now this guy was a really powerful dude—rich, politically connected, and ruthless. On the surface, it looked like he had me by the short hairs. But I don't bend over for guys like this. I fight back.

Instead of taking a by-the-book action like complaining to the officials or pleading with the guy, I decided I'd go vigilante style. I'd come at him in a way that he'd never expect. I'd knock him on his butt so hard he couldn't get up. There's an old saying: "If you don't like the heat, jump into the fire." I decided to jump.

The next day I set the wheels in motion for a stunt that nobody had ever pulled before in this sport, and, as far as I know, never, ever did again. I chose three bodybuilding magazines that had published articles on me and wrote each of them a letter, reporting *verbatim* what the AAU chairman had whispered to me that day after the show. I also put out a challenge: I would go on to win the nationals in the bodybuilding field, then come back and win the Mr. Florida—usually it was done the other way around—*despite* the chairman's threats.

All three magazines published my letter. These articles instantly caused a brouhaha in the bodybuilding community.

Overnight everyone in the sport was watching this guy and knew the kind of malicious crap he was capable of. As a judge he could no longer steal a show from me, or from anyone else. Too many people were looking at him now. I had knocked him on his rear, exposed him to his peers, and then, when I did in fact take the trophies at the nationals and the Mr. Florida (where he was a judge), I embarrassed him and his predictions in front of the world. Full Monty. Sometimes you have to fight for what you believe in.

"If at first the idea is not absurd, then there is no hope for it."

—*Albert Einstein, physicist*

Think "Improvement" as Well as "Original"

You don't have to reinvent the wheel to get beyond the box. Add a small improvement or adjustment that nobody else has thought of. Usually that's all you need. Sometimes it changes the world.

When motion pictures were first patented, their inventor, Thomas Edison, considered them a craze that would quickly pass.

Why?

Because the projected images were so wobbly and unsteady that the only thing viewers could see on the screen was a jumpy blur. To make matters worse, early film projectors put so much tension on the moving film that the sprocket holes were sometimes torn and even shredded to bits.

Perhaps Edison was right.

Then one day, as the story goes, a competitor of Edison's named Woodville Latham was studying a film projector in his lab. Watching as the celluloid roll wound its way through the machine's many gears and spools he was racking his brains on how to reduce tension on the film.

Suddenly an idea struck him.

It was ridiculously simple.

Could it be?

He reached out, pinched a length of the moving film, made a loop in it, and held the loop in place while the film continued to move through the projector.

Lo and behold, the loop released the tension on the film and the film started feeding effortlessly along the sprockets. The image on the screen improved immediately.

With a tiny modification, Latham had figured out a problem that even the great Edison had not been able to solve. In the process he had revolutionized the movie business and the world as well. Eventually he patented his invention. Today it is still known as the Latham Loop.

You don't always have to make a wonderful thing from scratch. Making a wonderful thing *better* can be sufficient. As the great architect and inventor Buckminster Fuller once remarked, "You can't change anything by fighting or resisting it. You change something by making it obsolete through superior methods."

"The real magic of discovery lies not in seeking new landscapes but in having new eyes."

—*Marcel Proust, French writer*

Time to Go Beyond

Where did I learn to think beyond the box? Where can you?

From a lot of amazing people.

From athletes, salespersons, CEOs, advertisers, celebrities, historical figures, your own neighbors—people who sense the limitations of linear A to B to C thinking, and who are willing to take that big leap of creativity that catapults them over the competition. Here are beyond-the-box stories that I think you'll find empowering, and that contain principles of creative thinking that can be applied to many life situations.

Jackie   After the early days of baseball when immortals like Ty Cobb and Honus Wagner ran the base paths without fear, the art of stealing home was put on hold. Managers in the 1940s and 1950s now became wary of taking risks and preferred to play the game by the odds, rarely letting even their fastest runners try this dangerous stunt.

Then along came Jackie Robinson.

Fresh up from the Negro Leagues, where risk was the name of the game, Robinson brought a secret weapon with him to the Brooklyn Dodgers. Armed with lightning speed (he had been a star running back on the UCLA football team) and, even more important, a built-in stealth meter to tell him when the time was right for audacious action, he began doing the unthinkable, stealing home time after time right under his opponents' noses. At the end of his career he had accomplished this awesome feat 19 times, a standard that no modern player has even come close to matching.

Out of the box. Beyond the box.

Build on the Old to Make the New   In 2003, still reeling from mistakes made during the "dot bomb" era, the Internet was filling up with web sites that did nothing much for anybody at all. Very few of these sites allowed users to connect with each other on a personal level. Almost none interfaced using photos, videos, music, blogs, and personal profiles.

All this changed when Brad Greenspan, president of eUniverse, came up with a simple outside-the-box idea that expanded on the model of an earlier web site, Friendster.

Why not give millions of people on the Web a way to meet new friends and greet old ones? Greenspan asked. Why not create a site where the latest juicy gossip can be exchanged, where family members can stay in touch, where new romantic contacts can be forged?

He named his new web site MySpace.

Employees at eUniverse were encouraged to hold contests to see who could sign up the most users. The many new personal features on MySpace made it popular overnight, and by the next year it had become the primo social networking site on the Internet.

Building on a prior model and giving it new wings, Greenspan had created something different and new.

See Things from Many Different Sides All at Once   Pablo Picasso developed his Cubist revolution in painting based on a new and mind-stretching principle.

For centuries Western artists had painted images in realistic terms. What you see is what you get. This was fine, Picasso told himself. But why stop here? Why portray an object on canvas from only one place in the room?

Instead, why not show an object from several angles *at the same time*? Depict a person's nose and eyes and chin simultaneously from three different viewpoints at once. Break up the flat plane into many smaller planes. Rearrange parts of a face, or a violin, or a bowl of fruit side by side. Go beneath the surface of things.

Picasso was one of the great beyond-the-box thinkers of all time.

When you're working out a new sales plan, a graphic design, or an improved service program, look at the problem from many different angles at once. Avoid limiting yourself to the garden-variety frontal view. Use your X-ray eyes to penetrate from behind, from the sides and corners. Break it up into many parts; then rearrange these parts into new patterns. Assemble outrageous combinations of images and concepts. Shuffle old ideas around like cards in a pack until you come up with a totally new hand. Soon you'll be viewing your world in Cubist terms. In the deal, you'll see many unique possibilities where others see just one—or none.

There's always a way!

Think Like a Child   Once I went to an art movie theater that was located in the basement of an office building. To get to the ticket booth you had to walk down a long, narrow corridor.

As it turned out, the janitor had mopped the floor of this corridor an hour or so before show time and had left his mop leaning diagonally across the narrow hallway. When the people in line (including myself) came to the mop they each stepped over it gingerly, some going to elaborate lengths not to touch the pole, as if something terrible would happen to them if they dared touch it.

Finally, a nine- or ten-year-old girl approached the mop. Instead of stepping over it like everyone else, she simply grabbed it and moved it out of the way, leaning it against the wall.

When this happened many of the people in line (including myself) started laughing. What a simple, elegant solution. Totally obvious. None of us sheep in the herd had the eyes to see it or the power of mind to conceive it. But the little girl did. There were no boxes in her head.

More Beyond the Boxers

Are you starting to see a pattern here, people? A way of approaching life and business?

In my own career, I spent several intense years during the 1990s selling the Gazelle Glider and other fitness machines on infomercials over the Home Shopping Network on TV. The machines did record-breaking numbers—over $1 billion in revenues.

But as the new millennium arrived, the sales figures started to dip. I began to realize that if I wanted to stay on top of the game, I needed to come up with something new and great.

I went to work and soon came up with a line of personal fitness aids that included a massager, a Rock n'Roll Stepper, personal trainer music CDs, health sandals, exercise sandals, postural pillows, inversion chairs, and several others. These new products lit up the phone lines at the television studio like crazy. The Rock n'Roll Stepper sold 37,000 units in one day on HSN. My Cheeks Sandals sold over 50,000 pairs.

Great! But I wanted to take sales a step further and to go beyond any box that had ever been placed on me. I was a lifestyle coach. This meant I not only wanted to exercise you right; I wanted to feed you right as well. Which meant I wanted to sell you *food*.

"Food!" the executives at the Home Shopping Network bellowed. "It's really hard to sell food on the Home Shopping Network, Tony! What kind of stuff are you talking about, anyway?"

"Energy drinks," I replied. "Meal replacement bars. Prepared high-protein and low-carb ready-made meals. Bison burgers."

"Bison! Are you freaking *nuts*?!"

Noooooo.

The first day I went on the air with my new product, bison hotdogs and burgers, I sold $1.4 million worth of them. These are still among the Home Shopping Network's best sellers today.

And speaking of HSN, you've already met Bud Paxson, owner of the Home Shopping Network and the man who got me started selling on TV. In 1982 Paxson owned a small AM radio station, WWQT 1470. He was barely selling enough advertising at the time to keep it solvent.

One day Paxson went to collect money owed him by one of his advertisers. But the advertiser was as broke as he was, and announced he couldn't make the payments.

This was bad. Without this money Paxson couldn't make payroll that week.

Instead of panicking, threatening to sue, or giving up, Paxson asked himself: What am I not seeing here? What solution is staring me in the face?

A remarkable idea came to him.

Contacting the deadbeat advertiser again, he told him that in place of the owed money he would accept any salable merchandise the advertiser happened to have in his store.

The advertiser replied that indeed he did have some interesting goods: avocado green can openers—112 of them, to be exact. (Why an advertiser would have so many green can openers in its back rooms Paxson didn't ask.)

"Send them over," Paxson said.

Then he did something totally off the charts.

Instructing one of his talk show hosts, Bob Circosta, to display these openers in an attractive way for the camera, he told Circosta to sell this merchandise *live* over the airways directly to the viewers at home. No one had ever thought of such a thing before.

To Paxson's astonishment, the audience response was fast and furious. All 112 avocado green can openers were sold out within an hour.

Sensing a remarkable new source of revenue waiting to be tapped, Paxson stepped even further into uncharted waters. Within the next year he and financier Roy Speer cofounded a cable television channel designed to sell a range of products *directly* to home viewers in Florida.

Three years later, in 1985, the station had raked in so much money that the two partners launched their channel nationwide. It was called the Home Shopping Network, and it was totally unlike anything anyone had ever seen in the business world—a brand-new, mind-bogglingly powerful selling instrument with the potential to reach a majority of people living on the planet. Over the years the network became a $3 billion business.

It pays to think in ways that others don't.

A last story that I really get a kick out of reached me via the grapevine some years ago. It may be an urban legend for all I know, but it illustrates the art of thinking beyond the box in as clear and bold a way as I've ever heard.

A Mexican trader started crossing the United States–Mexico border every morning with a large sack of sundries piled in his wheelbarrow. Word soon went out among the American authorities that the trader was smuggling something illegal into the States and back again to Mexico. Nobody could figure out what it was.

From this time on whenever the trader arrived at the checkpoint, a certain customs inspector was assigned to search the trader's pack inside and out. But no matter how hard the inspector looked, nothing suspicious ever turned up.

This cat-and-mouse game went on for many years. In the process the trader and the customs inspector became buddies. One day on his way back across the Mexican border, the trader, wheeling his wheelbarrow, sought the custom inspector out, told her he was retiring, and that this was probably the last time they would meet. He'd come to say good-bye.

The inspector was sad. But she was also curious.

"Come on," she said. "We're old friends. I won't rat you out. We know you're been smuggling *something* all this time. What is it?"

"You're right," the trader said. "I have."

"So what is it?"

He turned around without answering, walked till he crossed the border into Mexico, then looked back at his old friend.

"Wheelbarrows!" he shouted.

Classic beyond-the-box thinking. There's always a way.

Tony's Takeaways

What is a box?

Box: "A four-sided container designed to hold things in."

Box: "A square or rectangle."

Box: "A sealed cubicle."

Box: "A small structure serving as a covering."

Box: "A receptacle with four sides, a bottom, and a cover designed to contain objects or perishables."

Box: "A cage or prison."

Box: "A predicament; as in *a tight box*."

Which box are you in? Which box are you thinking beyond?

Tony's Seven Tips for Innovative Thinking

1. Imagine that you're in prison and you want to break out. The tools you have at your disposal are your reason, your intuition,

your ambition, and your creative imagination. If you put all of them to work for you all at once, no jail in the world can hold you.

2. If you come up with a good concept, don't stop there. Keep working on it until it's a *great* concept. Then push beyond that till it's an unbelievably *fantastic* concept.

3. Try it out. See how it works. If it's good, make it even better. If it's as good as you can do, start selling it right away.

4. Genius is the ability to take a good idea and multiply it a thousand times.

5. Good ideas do grow on trees. They're known as fruit.

6. There's no end to your creativity and your powers of imagination. They are totally without limit. They open out to the universe. Remember that.

7. If you want a totally new answer, look first to the obvious. It's often the last thing people notice.

Out of the Box with John D.

John D. Rockefeller was arguably the most successful American entrepreneur of all time. Starch-collared, honest, fussy, in his youth he worked as an assistant bookkeeper for a produce-shipping company in Cleveland, a city that boasted one of the country's few oil refineries. It was the mid-1800s and it seemed that everyone had a case of oil drilling fever. Thousands of people were pouring into Texas, Pennsylvania, and other oil-rich states trying their luck with rigs. The trouble was that most wells never produced and drillers were going broke right and left.

Using his business savvy, Rockefeller assessed the situation and came up with a totally new approach to the oil business.

He noted that petroleum-based products like kerosene were shipping with increasing regularity. Putting two and two together, he realized that there were millions of dollars to be made in drilling oil, yes. But there were far fewer risks and just as much profit to be made in refining it and even more profit to be made *in transporting it from place to place*.

He built his own refinery, set up his own petroleum delivery systems, and the rest is history.

No boxes for Rockefeller.

7

You Gotta Step Out to Stand Out

"I never try to fit in. I was born to stand out."

—T-shirt slogan

"Look at me! Look at me! Look at me!"

—T-shirt slogan

"There is no such thing as bad publicity. Only publicity."

—Anonymous

"In Hollywood, an equitable divorce settlement means each party getting 50 percent of the publicity."

—Lauren Bacall, actress

"Publicity can be terrible. But only if you don't get any."

—Jane Russell, actress

You Gotta Step Out to Stand Out

How to Step Out of the Chorus Line

Every red-blooded American, young and old, knows the TV show *I Love Lucy* and its zany heroine, played by actress, Lucille Ball. They know the show firsthand, having watched it every Monday night from 1951 to 1957. Or they know it secondhand from viewing its endless late night reruns.

What many people old and young do *not* know is that Lucille Ball began her career not as a comedienne but as a model for the Chesterfield Cigarette Girl, then as a Broadway showgirl, and finally as a member of film producer Samuel Goldwyn's crew of female dancers, known as the "Goldwyn Girls."

In the role of song and dance lady, Lucy was just one pretty face in a crowd of drop-dead gorgeous chorus girls, all of them, like herself, panting for stardom. The problem was, how could she hook the attention of her boss, Sam Goldwyn, and get him to remember her long enough to win a talking role in one of his movies?

Lucy thought about this challenge for some time and finally hit on a bold strategy that would make her stand out from the crowd.

Sam Goldwyn, she learned, was scheduled that week to meet in his office with a group of contract writers to discuss a new film project. When the hour of the meeting arrived, Lucy drove her car onto the studio lot, parked it in front of the building where the meeting was taking place, and started to honk her horn.

At first Goldwyn and his writers ignored the clamor. But Lucy kept at it, honking away full blast.

Finally Goldwyn walked over to the window, opened it, looked down, and saw Lucy smiling up at him. About to scold her for making so much noise, Lucy beat him to the punch. "Can the writers come out and play with me now, Mr. Goldwyn?" she called up to him, batting her famous long eyelashes and smiling her best movie star smile.

Goldwyn closed the window in annoyance. But like it or not, Lucy had made an impression on him that he would not soon forget.

Several months later a small role for a dumb blond type came up in one of his films, and Goldwyn began searching his stable for the right performer. In the process he remembered that ditzy Lucille Ball who'd tried to honk her way into his attention. She looked the part, all right. And she certainly must have the ambition to play it. Why not? he thought to himself, and gave Lucy the role.

And so, by taking a chance, by being gutsy and inventive, by stepping out to stand out, Lucille Ball created film history, launching herself into a career that would one day make her the all-time queen of American TV comedy. Moral: You have to step out to stand out.

"Those who are blessed with the most talent don't necessarily outperform everyone else. It's the people with follow-through who excel."

—Mary Kay Ash, entrepreneur

Learn the Power of Small Steps

Bodybuilding shows are organized like Miss America contests.

Imagine a stage full of tanned, hyped-up, half-naked young Samsons all lined up in rows waiting to perform under the spotlight, each so perfectly built that it's practically impossible for audiences—or judges—to tell them apart.

When you find yourself up there with a pack of amazing muscle muffins like these, your problem is pretty clear: How do I stand out from the crowd?

I myself wasn't all *that* well built. Just a well-muscled, well-defined, healthy-looking young guy with a shitload of motivation who approached this challenge and every one like it with one thought in mind: "You have to step out to stand out."

In this case, "stepping out" meant *literally* stepping out of line.

In the Mr. Florida contest, to explain what I mean, I was on stage with 179 other young bulls, each waiting his turn to perform in the ring. The audience and judges were scanning us up and down, taking in this mass of brawn, but not zeroing in on anyone in particular. To get the edge, I needed everyone there to instantly focus their attention *on me!* I wanted to win this contest in the minds of the judges *before the judging actually took place.*

Was this possible? Yes, but only if I did something so outrageous they'd have no choice but to single me out.

The solution came in a flash. Yeah, baby! There's always a way.

While standing in the line of contestants I abruptly, and for no apparent reason, took several steps forward, hung there for a few seconds, then stepped back.

A few minutes later I did the same thing.

After a couple of forwards and backwards, the judges started getting steamed, and they addressed me over the PA. "Number 15, we can see you. We *assure you*, we can see you! Please step back in line!"

Fantastic! They're talking *to* me! They're looking *at* me! And so is everybody else in the house! A few moments earlier I was just one of 180 faces. Now I'm the *only* face.

I then took further advantage of the edge I'd grabbed by smiling at the judges, winking, wiggling, all the while pointing to the number on my posing trunks and nodding my head yes. Yes, me! I'm your winner! You've got no choice in the matter!

Me!

"Be different, stand out, and work your butt off."

—*Reba McEntire, country and western singer*

The Goldest Is the Boldest

Even before the Mr. Florida meet took place that year I'd already taken "stand out" steps to win in advance.

Most bodybuilding contestants at the time were using the same commercial self-tanners like Man Tan and Tanorama to give their torsos color, shine, and muscle definition. These cheapo oils turned the skin a nasty orangish brown. Picture a hundred muscle men crowded together on stage, all blending into one huge orangish blur.

To improve on this look—and to make sure I got singled out—I started using a women's tanning cream marketed by Estée Lauder. This high-end product gave my torso a rich, golden color that drew all the judges' eyes in my direction. When I walked on stage I looked golden, in contrast to 179 dull orange torsos. One judge confided in me later on that he couldn't keep his eyes off me. He and the other judges, he said, had singled me out as the winner the moment I walked onstage.

Then there was the music.

A week before the show I tape-recorded a message, repeating my name and show number over and over. I then added this message at a *subliminal level* to the musical sound track I'd recorded for my routine. When my time came to perform and my music was switched on, this message was broadcast again and again directly into the judges' subconscious minds: "Pick Tony Little, number 15. Pick Tony Little, number 15. Pick Tony Little, number 15. . . ."

After the show several of the judges complimented me: "Great music, Tony!"

"Let us carefully observe those good qualities wherein our enemies excel us; and endeavor to excel them, by avoiding what is faulty, and imitating what is excellent in them."

—*Plutarch, Roman historian*

Who Are These Guys?!

Remember the classic late 1960s film *Butch Cassidy and the Sundance Kid*? When Butch and Sundance rob a train, and end up getting chased by a relentless posse? No matter what they do to shake them, the posse sticks close on their trail. Not used to such dogged pursuit, Butch and Sundance keep turning in their saddles and asking each other the same question: "Who *are* those guys?!"

"Each one of you has something no one else has, or has ever had: your fingerprints, your brain, your heart. Be an individual. Be unique. Stand out. Make noise. Make someone notice. That's the power of individuals."

—*Jon Bon Jovi, rock musician*

That's what I want people to ask about me. "Who is this guy?" And that's what I want people to ask about you.

By the way, stepping out does not necessarily mean bragging. Don't get the two confused. When I step out I'm making a statement about who I am, what I do, how good I am at what I do, and what I'm prepared to do *for you.* As baseball great Dizzy Dean remarked, "If you can do it, it ain't bragging."

The great motivational writer and speaker Tony Robbins once swung his six-feet-seven frame down onto a stage hanging on to a 30-foot rope. Gets your attention, right? For added mileage, it subliminally builds admiration for Robbins's daring and physical strength, and helps you trust him.

That's stepping out.

In my own TV selling program I'll do crazy stuff to capture viewers' interest and to show them why my product is so good. I'll drop a bowling ball on my posture pillow to display how resilient it is. I'll jump up and down on a competitor's pillow to show how crappily it's made. I'll put a fake human skull on top of my pillow to demonstrate how snugly it fits. I'll jump into a pillowcase and hop around to show how strong the fabric is. On one show I danced with a skeleton.

Off-the-charts craziness, but viewers get a laugh out of it, which is cool. More important, they remember these visual stunts long after they've forgotten my actual words.

Dale Carnegie, perhaps the greatest of all personal motivators, tells in his classic book, *How to Win Friends and Influence People,* how as a young man he went from store to store selling cash registers. Visiting a food market one day, he saw that the registers at the checkout counter were defective and seriously outdated. Approaching the owner, Carnegie told the man he was literally throwing pennies away every time one of his customers went through the pay line.

As he said these words, he threw a handful of pennies onto the floor.

"He quickly became more attentive," writes Carnegie. "The mere words should have been of interest to him, but the sound of pennies hitting the floor really stopped him. I was able to get an order from him to replace all of his old machines."

Dale stepping out.

In a recent article in *People* magazine on film great Elizabeth Taylor's famous jewel collection, the onetime "most famous woman in the world" remarked, "I can't remember a time when people did not associate me with diamonds. And really, if you're going to have a signature, why not make sure it sparkles?"

Elizabeth stepping out.

Every year Macy's Department Store sponsors a Thanksgiving parade that trades on its name: the Macy's Thanksgiving Day Parade. This New York City tradition has taken place since 1924, and today it attracts more than 3.4 million viewers. Just by associating its name with a beloved event, and by turning the phrase "Macy's Thanksgiving Day Parade" into a household term, Macy's has positioned itself as the most famous department store in the United States.

That's stepping out to stand out.

"Either dance well or quit the ballroom."

—*Greek proverb*

Use Whatever Works

Publicity stunts are great examples of calling attention to yourself and *away* from the competition.

Harrods department store in London once rolled out more than 600 meters of fancy paper to gift wrap a helicopter for one of its high-end customers.

In 1959 the Guinness Brewery Company wanted to branch out from its Irish customer base and give its ale a global identity. In those environmentally brain-dead times, the company dropped 150,000 Guinness Ale bottles into the Atlantic and Caribbean oceans. Inside each bottle was a set of instructions on how to convert the bottle into a lamp.

Within five years Guinness was a worldwide name.

GoldenPalace.com, an online gambling web site working out of the Caribbean, has used several outrageous step-out stunts in the past few years to drive traffic to its site.

One of their attention grabbers was to buy William Shatner's kidney stone for $25,000, and to auction it off for charity. Another was to pay people to tattoo the GoldenPalace logo on certain sensitive body parts. Their most famous boondoggle was to purchase a partially eaten grilled cheese sandwich with the likeness of the Virgin Mary toasted into it for $28,000.

Extreme? Well, yeah. But it sure gets people looking.

An article published on the Bobbermarketing.com web site explains how the Ford Motor Company chose the *Oprah Winfrey Show* to showcase the launch of the new Focus model. Early in the program, the site reports, Oprah started talking up the fact that *someone* in the audience was going to win the keys to a new Focus that morning. She told audience members to look under their seats for a box with a key in it.

Everyone did.

And everyone came up with a key.

It turned out that each person in the audience was awarded a new Ford Focus for their very own that day! In turn, Ford got millions of dollars' worth of publicity for the price of a few hundred car giveaways, and Oprah was credited in the press for being the world's most generous woman.

"You can do the same thing," writes Bobbermarketing.com. "Set up a seminar or workshop with a vendor that has a new product coming out. Tease potential attendees by hinting that someone in the audience would land one of the new, yet-to-be-released products free. At the end of the seminar, announce that everyone in the audience gets the product free."

Go Ahead, Try It

There are a lot of tricks I recommend to people who ask me how to stand out.

I tell them to use anything you can to make yourself a little different, a little more interesting, a little more provocative.

For example, if everyone in your office wears casual clothes, come to work in a tie and jacket. Or vice versa. People notice. Step out to stand out.

When you give presentations, do it with a twist. If others present silent slide shows, use music or voice-over. If people illustrate their text with photos, use animation. If the ladies down the corridor use a 15-inch laptop, bring in a 40-inch screen.

Does everyone at your workplace carry their papers in a tan attaché case? Carry yours in a brightly colored purse or shoulder bag. Go out and buy yourself a seriously expensive computer case. Bring it to meetings and display it on the table in front of you for all to see. Use a Montblanc fountain pen instead of a standard ballpoint when taking notes. When lunching with colleagues at a restaurant, use whatever smattering of Italian or French or Spanish you have to order. Knowledge of foreign languages always impresses.

Incorporate memorable extras into your sales repertoire. Hand out a ridiculously eye-popping business card. Advertise in up-and-coming magazines and journals that the rest of the trade is ignoring. Print a brochure in black and white when everyone else is using flashy colors.

When you meet a business client for the first time, exploit the moment. A colleague of mine does this by saying odd things when she first shakes hands with a new client. Things like, "I'll always remember this moment," or "I'll never let you or your company down." The clients don't exactly know what to make of these slightly off-center statements. But they sure as heck remember the woman who said them.

How often do you have a great idea during a business sitdown, but you're too timid or unsure to blurt it out? You're not convinced that your colleagues will approve of what you say, or agree with it.

Hey, I'm here to tell you, folks: Blurt it out! Even if the gang at the table doesn't like what you say, you'll make a lot more impact than if you just sit there the whole meeting blending in with the wallpaper.

Step out to stand out.

There's always a way.

Sometimes You Need Shoes to Step Out

I recently heard a story from a telemarketer I know about a young loan agent who was trying to make contact with a number of real estate agencies in her area.

Rather than cold call or cold knock on doors, the woman went out and bought five pairs of inexpensive women's shoes. Inside each shoe she wrote, "Hi, I'm Barbara Lehman, a loan agent, and I'm trying to 'get my foot in the door' with your agency. I'll be back to meet you tomorrow."

She dropped off one shoe at 10 different real estate agencies in the area.

Kind of crazy, huh? But not so crazy. How can you not notice a woman's shoe with a message in it sitting in front of your office door? And how can some part of you, at least, not be impressed by the stunt's ingenuity?

As promised, Barbara did come back the next day to all 10 agencies, where she made a number of solid contacts. To this day when people see her they say, "Hey, you're the woman with the shoes, right?"

Keep in mind that stepping out and getting noticed means taking risks. Risks get you seen, heard, and talked about, even if they don't always pan out. Even if they fall flat on their face. Better to have risked and lost than never to have risked at all.

When I was a kid my mother used to tell me, "Guts take you further than knowledge, money, or power."

You've got to have guts to stand out.

Yep, Drop Names!

There's a taboo you come across sometimes in the business world against dropping names. For reasons I don't quite get, it's considered tacky to mention the celebrated or significant people you've known or worked with during your career.

I say: *Forgetaboutit!*

Dropping names is one of the best ways I know of stepping out.

Dropping names means taking advantage of your most impressive experiences to impress others and make the sale. What's wrong with that? Drop a name or an achievement in the right context, and people look at you in a different way. They may even know you're doing it intentionally. So? The fact that you associated with a well-known personality or were involved in an awesome achievement still has a potent effect on people's opinions of you. And that's all you want to do—make a positive impression to help your cause. (Just don't drop the same names at your next meeting.)

I know one guy who's worked as a salesman for several major computer companies, including Microsoft and IBM. Despite his amazing resume, he was having trouble finding a job. He came to me for advice.

"What do you tell interviewers?" I asked him.

"Basically, I wait for them to ask me a question," he replied. "Then I answer it."

"Yo, that's it in a nutshell," I said. "You can't wait for the interviewer to ask you the exact perfect question each time. You've got to take control of the interview immediately and front-load it with your best credentials. I mean, if you've worked for all these big companies, let the interviewer know about it in the first 60 seconds. Give them the best of your bio right away—about helping out the CEO at XYZ company, about being on the team that developed this amazing storage system, about working with an important Japanese money guy from Panasonic, about getting advice from Bill Gates—whatever. Let these stories position you as someone in the know and out of the ordinary. This way the interviewer—or the business associate, client, or lunch partner—knows you're a heavy hitter and treats you accordingly."

There are a million ways to step out in business and in life. The important thing is to *remember* to step out, and then to *do* it. Keep your eye out for opportunities. Don't be afraid of criticism, or taking risks, or seeming a little outlandish. The squeaky wheel gets oiled. As the great song-and-dance man George M. Cohan once advised, "Whatever you do, do it with a little dressing!"

There's always a way.

Tony's Takeaways

- Even if you're afraid to step out, do it anyway. Sometimes we have to force ourselves to be great.
- You usually won't lose by being bold. And if you do, well, at least you've been bold, and that has its own rewards.
- Learn to use your fear as a fuel that energizes you to move forward, not as a chain that holds you back.
- When you step out, stay out. If you don't have to step back, don't.
- The bolder the statement you make, the bigger the impression you leave. If you're going to step out, step out all the way.

8

Self-Brand Your Way to Success

"I've never lived in a building without my name on it."

—*Ivanka Trump, model and businesswoman*

"At a formal dinner a lady was sitting next to Raymond Loewy, the father of industrial design. They struck up a conversation.

'Why,' the woman inquired, 'did you put two Xs in the Exxon logo?'

'Why are you asking?' he wanted to know.

'Because,' she said, 'I can't help noticing it.'

'Well,' he replied, 'that's your answer.'"

—*Alan Fletcher, graphic designer, in his book*
The Art of Looking Sideways

"When you think of the blur of all the brands that are out there, the ones you believe in and the ones you remember, like Chanel and Armani, are the ones that stand for something. Fashion is about establishing an image that consumers can adapt to their own individuality. And it's an image that can change, that can evolve. It doesn't reinvent itself every two years."

—*Ralph Lauren, fashion designer*

Self-Brand Your Way to Success

All You'll Ever Need to Know about Self-Branding

Madonna, Eminem, Elvis, Oprah—they're all just first names, but first names that have been burned into your consciousness so deeply that when I mention them you instantly know who I'm talking about.

The same principle holds true with everyday products like Tupperware, Xerox, Scotch tape, Kleenex. The brand name becomes the generic name for the object itself—plastic containers, machine copies, transparent tape, tissues. This is the real definition of a successful brand—*instant recognition*.

A female Elvis impersonator from Las Vegas was recently quoted in *Time* magazine as saying, "The magic word is Elvis, Elvis, Elvis. Elvis is my life, the very core of me."

That, my friends, is branding with a vengeance. And brand recognition is 75 percent of selling.

A brand is valuable because it presells your product. If the brand is persuasive and persistent, customers will already have an upscale opinion of it. When they see it on the shelf they will instantly recognize it, and their hand will reach for it. Almost automatically.

Suppose you see a widget in a store with "As Seen on Television" printed on the package. Half the selling work is already done. The name gives you a sense of confidence and familiarity. Just to know that the product appeared on TV makes it authentic, real, official. It's part of mainstream American life. Therefore, you think, it must be good. I'll buy it.

Whenever you can, brand yourself and brand your product.

If you mention the name Tony Little to the man or woman on the street, they may know who you're talking about or they may not. But go ahead, describe that guy on TV infomercials or TV shopping with the blond ponytail and baseball cap working himself into a frenzy on an exercise machine and yelling, "You can do it!" and "Conceive, believe, achieve!" When they hear this description, chances are my image will automatically pop up in their minds and they'll know who you're talking about.

The operative term I'm using here is *image*. "Image is all," as advertisers insist. To manufacture a memorable one for myself, I've put two of my most conspicuous personal assets to work: my appearance and my voice.

For example, when I'm selling things on TV I dress in a variety of wearing apparel, including skintight shirts, spandex shorts, bright-colored shoes and matching watch, funny hats, boa constrictor skin boots, drill sergeant fatigues—anything to catch the eye and make an impression. I'm always smiling, jumping, talking fast, popping out my eyes. I play inspirational music. During a shoot I surround myself with eye-catching, healthy-looking female demonstrators who have fun personalities. I do a lot of playful, energetic interactions with them, many of which I don't know I'm going to do until I do them.

In short, I establish such a striking visual image in the minds of viewers that after seeing me once or twice they never forget me.

The same holds true with my voice.

I don't talk in that hale and hearty tone of the typical fitness trainer. I'm in your face, one-on-one. I put a lot of feeling in my voice, a lot of energy, passion, and enthusiasm. I modulate its sound up and down. My voice startles people, energizes them, gets them listening whether they like it or not. Shock and awe. People don't suddenly yell at you out of the blue on a commercial. So I do. That's what projects my message—energy and passion. I make jokes—loudly. I do dumb things—meaningfully. I never go by a script. I wing it. It's all part of getting viewers' emotions flowing and making a lasting impression.

"Mr. Little says he has carefully honed his image as America's Personal Trainer," an article about me in the *New York Times* explained.

"A stickler for detail and a master of self-promotion, he has so completely entwined his image with that of his product line that the shrewdest concept developed by Mr. Little may not be the tapes or the books . . . but Tony Little himself."

There's a scene in the movie *Juno* where a guy notices an exercise machine sitting in the corner of the room, and says to this woman something like, Hey, my wife exercises on a machine like this with that crazy guy on TV, Tony Little. What a nut! I don't think he's all there!

Why do people resonate with this scene in the film? Because they're responding to the Tony Little brand I've impressed on their minds, to the persona I've made for myself as the mad, overcaffeinated, late-night TV fitness evangelist. It's almost Pavlovian. Say ponytail and baseball cap, talk about exercise machines, and an image of Tony Little comes on your mental screen.

"A brand name is more than a word. It is the beginning of a conversation."

—Advertising aphorism

Look, if I ask you what the moon's made of, you answer instantly: green cheese. Right?

If I say, "You deserve a break today at _____" you automatically fill in the word "McDonald's." When I say "_____ Ready to fly when you are," you immediately think "Delta." It's a conditioned reflex. An automatic response.

That's how you build a brand.

How to Sell Yourself *and* Your Product

Maybe you'll never become a brand name on TV.

But you *can* brand your name and reputation deep into your customers' minds. You *can* make yourself so recognizable and distinctive in your business community that others buy you, and business naturally flows your way.

Start by practicing the methods I gave you in the preceding chapter. Call attention to yourself in an interesting or outlandish way. Talk yourself up. Take chances. Be assertive. Be creative. Be inventive. Be poles apart. Cultivate personal identity markers that make you stand out like a single red dot on a field of yellow dots.

"Your brand represents your business identity," writes Steven D. Strauss in *The Small Business Bible* (John Wiley & Sons, 2005), "your unique position in the market. Are you the friendly lawyer, the holistic market, the geeky computer consultant, or what? Without a brand, you may find that instead of being all things to all people, you are nothing to no one."

In the renowned Broadway musical *Gypsy*, three aging burlesque strippers perform a song-and-dance number in which each explains her formula for success. One stripper's secret is to light up her hooters while she dances. Another's is to bend over and blow a trumpet through her legs. That gets them watching. A third flaps a set of butterfly wings while she strips.

Three different routes to "stardom." But they all agree on one thing. If you're going to succeed, "You gotta have a gimmick!"

And you do, too. Gimmick is another way of saying self-branding, of standing out in the crowd.

One executive I know had a special logo seal made for herself with her initials engraved on it. She uses the seal to stamp all her letters and memos. Whenever a client or colleague receives correspondence from her they immediately recognize her seal, and remember her. That's a branding gimmick that works.

If you own your own company, give it a zany or unusual name. Or go ahead, name it after yourself. This tried-and-true method personalizes a business, makes it homey, and links your identity with whatever goods or services you offer. Think Famous Amos, Trader Joe's, Norton AntiVirus, Ford Motor, Colonel Sanders, Chef

Boyardee, Perdue Farms chicken, Ralph Lauren, and hundreds of other biggies.

Many of the people who founded these companies or run them feature pictures of themselves on their products. This is smart. They're selling a smiling face and dynamic personality along with a name. They understand that people are more likely to buy if they know the person they're buying from. Think of how real estate people put photos of themselves next to their listings.

"When the idea came up [for the Newman's Own brand]," wrote actor Paul Newman, "I said, 'Are you crazy? Stick my face on the label of salad dressing?' And then, of course, we got the whole idea of exploitation and how circular it is. Why not, really, go to the fullest length, and the silliest length, in exploiting yourself and turn the proceeds back to the community?"

"A sign of celebrity is that a man's name is worth more than his service."

—Daniel Boorstin, American historian

Many of the printed materials I send out of my office, like brochures, letters, and advertising, include photographs of me, some serious, some hamming it up. Potential buyers are far more likely to respond to faces than to facelessness. Personalizing sells!

Still another branding gimmick is to identify yourself with a unique or striking fashion style.

I know one young salesman who wears a white linen handkerchief tucked neatly in his jacket pocket whenever he makes a sales call. It's so old-fashioned it's hip! People call him the "handkerchief boy," and they know exactly who he is when he comes knocking.

Another PR woman I work with always dresses in red—something different to make her stand out. Let your own personal style do the walking and talking and selling for you.

There's always a way.

Don't Be Bland, Be a Brand

In his book *The Brand Called You* (McGraw-Hill, 2008), media expert Peter Montoya provides 265 pages of outstanding methods for self-branding. Give it a look. (I must admit I have a silent agenda here. The book contains a "Brand Case Study" of me.)

Montoya points out that in the United States any candidate for public or political office knows that "you as candidate must define yourself before your *opponent* defines you."

To accomplish this feat you gotta be proactive and take control of your image before others take control of it for you. Being proactive means constructing a strong business identity. It means not allowing yourself to be typecast by clients or competitors. "By defining yourself in the minds of your prospects instead of letting them define you," Montoya writes, "your brand attracts new business to your door, so you spend less time doing business development, and more time servicing clients."

Here are some of the self-branding strategies I've used in the past 20 years to stay proactive. They're not as dramatic as yelling at TV viewers while riding the wild Gazelle, but they're you know, practical and effective.

- **Let print material trumpet your name.** Your brochure, your sales letters, your stationery, your card, your letterhead, your memos, your logo—everything that leaves your desk or your shop should bear the stamp of your business personality.

  In my own office, as I mentioned, many of the letters and promotional materials we send out feature my picture along with several high-recognition motivational slogans. Brand, brand, brand! Use printed material to tell the buying public what's standout about you and your service. Use it as a tool to communicate who you are, and to explain the groovy benefits you offer. Use it to show how your product will make customers' lives happier, healthier, and richer.

- **Send out an e-mail letter.** Do you have unique information that can help your clients? Is there a list of customers you need to stay in touch with on a regular basis? Are you interested in updating clients on new offerings? If yes to any of these, consider sending out a monthly e-mail letter. The price is right—nothing—and if you or your staff members have time to compose it, this branding channel is a potent way of getting your name before the public eye.

    The web site www.streamsend.com will get you up and running in e-mail marketing. Take a look, too, at www.constantcontact.com and www.mailchimp.com. The web site www.majon.com offers a number of get-started e-mail services, plus an expensive but useful piece of e-mail software called Web Traffic Builder.

- **Show off your great web site.** If you're in business for yourself, consider hiring a web site designer to make you a seriously amazing web site. Your site should have visual sparkle, be easy to navigate, and have a superprofessional look to it. An eye-catching site drives traffic to your cyber doorstop. Use it to make business allies and to link with other sites. If you're in sales, a good site brings in leads. Use it as a platform to create a blog to provide special knowledge only you have in your field of specialization. Give the site a great name, too. Visit a web domain registration site like www.register.com or www.yourname.com, and look around. There are still plenty of great names out there, though they're running out quickly.

- **Learn from other web sites.** While you're at it, take a look at my own page, www.tonylittle.com. It's a prototype for self-branding. Visitors are welcomed with a sound track of my signature (and self-branding) slogan "You can do it!" They're entertained with a montage of photographs of me as bodybuilder, salesman, TV personality, and personal trainer. We feature success stories from people who've used my products, product information, purchase forms, and a "Tony's Gym" department where visitors can ask questions, learn new exercise techniques, and get helpful advice. I update my site frequently and make it as friendly as possible. In short, I use this super-powerful tool to push my personal brand.

- **Take advantage of social networks on the Internet.** Start a blog or web log. Put your name, your picture, your pro-file, and your work history on a popular social networking site like www.digg.com, www.myspace.com, http://technorati.com, www.zing.com, www.youtube, www.care2.com, www.twitter.com, or www.facebook.com. You can even create your own social net-work and use it for business purposes (go to www.ning.com for information). Social networking, if done tastefully and thought-fully, is a terrific way to meet people in your profession. It lets you express your professional views, make contacts, and keep a high profile before your business peers. Many social networking medi-ums offer a chance to join special-interest groups, and to interact with men and women in your field of specialization. Social media and networking sites are also being used more and more to attract quality traffic to web sites.

- **Specialize.** Specialization, Peter Montoya, insists, is the single most important personal branding strategy in your arsenal. "You sim-ply cannot build an effective brand," Montoya writes, "without being a specialist. . . . Specializing lets you pick a few lucrative, in-demand areas of your business and build your brand around them. Specialization offers many important benefits to any business."

- **Make your place of work stand out.** This branding principle can be applied on the smallest possible scale and the largest. If you're a single employee or a one-person operation, check out your office workspace—the pictures on your desk, the blinds, the rugs, the office chair. Can they be upgraded? Can they be made to emphasize the importance of your business history and personality? If you have a private office, what can you do to make it a showcase of who you are and what you offer? Consider filling your waiting room with interesting pictures, stuff on shelves, and framed diplomas that pound home your great credentials. Consider painting your office a distinctive color or filling it with furniture that people remember. You should see my office—fun, casual, different. The place where you work can be made into a brand unto itself.

- **Keep a high profile in your community.** Meeting people and making social contacts is a great way to self-brand. Rev your rep up. Make people notice you. Get a reputation for integrity, honesty, and hard work. People will remember. Offer a college scholarship. Join a local civic organization like the Lions Club or Kiwanis. Give seminars and classes. Hold special events. Lecture at the local high school or college. Get yourself elected to the board of a local charity or simply work there. It's good for you and for the people you help. Arrange to be interviewed on local radio or TV. Sponsor a charity or a local sports team. Let people know you're around, and that you're an active member of your community. People will recognize you, remember you, call you, hire you, and buy what you're selling.

"Gene Simmons of the rock band KISS once remarked that although he liked being in a rock-and-roll band, he loved being a rock-and-roll *brand.* What did he mean by that? Think about KISS for a moment. What images and feelings come to mind? Probably that distinctive KISS logo, the white makeup, the outrageous shows, the wild stories. KISS carefully cultivated that billion-dollar bad-boy image, and it's worth a fortune to them. That is what Simmons meant: Having a band is great, but it's the brand that pays the bills."

—*Steven D. Strauss, in* The Small Business Bible

The Long Arm of a Personal Brand

Sometimes people's personal brands can be deceptive or even play with your head.

Think of George Washington. His brand is deeply lodged in the minds of all Americans: an elderly, stern-looking aristocrat in a classic white wig. Unmistakable self-branding. The only thing is, in real life Washington had wooden teeth and red hair. Or Attila the Hun. When you picture this bloody conqueror, you think of a giant barbarian swinging a club. In reality, Attila the Hun was a midget. Cary Grant, one of the most self-branded film actors of all time, once made a revealing remark. "Everybody wants to be Cary Grant," he said. "Even *I* want to be Cary Grant."

"A personal brand creates expectations in the minds of others of what they'll get when they work with you. If you can figure out what your target market values are, and create a brand that promises to deliver that value again and again, prospects will beat down your door and burn up your phone lines. The catch: you've got to deliver on that promise 100 percent of the time."

—*Peter Montoya, media expert and author of The Brand Called You*

I once took a business trip to the Tonga Islands near Fiji to help train the King of Tonga. That's a whole other story. Anyway, while I was there I stayed at a hotel where the laundry facility was pretty crappy. I started bringing my shirts to a dry cleaner a few blocks down the street.

The elderly Tonganese gentleman behind the counter, though he spoke passable English, was stern and grumpy. I brought my shirts to him several times during my stay, and each time I barely received a nod.

Finally, a day or so before I was scheduled to leave the country, I picked up my shirts from his store for the last time and started to walk out of the shop.

"Hey, mister, mister!" the old gentleman called out after me.

I turned, surprised and puzzled.

"Yes?"

"YOU CAN DO IT!" he yelled, still not smiling. Then he turned and walked to the back of the store without another word.

Such is the power of the self-brand.

9

The Greatest Selling Secret of All Time

The Greatest Selling Secret of All Time

How to Succeed in Business by Really Trying

I'll tell you right now the greatest selling secret in the world. It's perseverance.

That's right.

Drive.

Pushiness.

Persistence.

Willpower.

Stick-to-itiveness.

Determination.

Never take no for an answer.

Always say yes when you answer.

Never quit.

Never say die.

Die when you say never.

Keep at 'em, dude.

Go get 'em, baby!

Am I kidding you?

I don't think so.

People, this is the *one* asset that every man and woman in the world of business and commerce absolutely *must have* for success.

I don't just mean your proverbial foot-in-the-door type of salesperson, either. I mean men and women in all fields of business and life who are trying to get ahead and fulfill their dreams. This is the secret. This is it. Develop perseverance and you'll become a richer, happier, more successful individual. Ignore it and you'll approach every task in business and in life with two hands tied behind your back.

Remember how in a chemistry experiment you add two or three chemicals to a lab beaker and nothing changes? Then you add a fourth chemical, the catalyst, and suddenly the other chemicals turn green, or fizz, or blow up the school. This is what perseverance is: It's the key ingredient that makes all the parts of a plan come together, and that drives this plan to success.

I know this to be true from many experiences in my own life. Persistence has kept me moving ahead in the face of humongous obstacles until my determination finally gets me to *win*. If I hadn't had this *one quality* I'd still be cleaning gyms somewhere or watching TV in a studio apartment. To be honest with you, I might even be dead.

That's how important perseverance has been in my own personal and professional life.

That's how important it should be in yours.

"Success is going from failure to failure without losing enthusiasm."

—Danny Glover, American actor

Per-Sis-Tense

What would you think of a woman who was so relentlessly focused on having her poems published that she sent in a different set of verses to the same 10 magazines every month for over 20 years? And every month she received 10 rejection slips.

After six or seven years, if you were her friend, wouldn't you tell her to think about getting a day job?

Well, if you'd told that to Gertrude Stein in 1915, she would have given you a quick smile, and kept right on penning verses. When she died in 1946 she was considered one of America's greatest poets.

Think about the following words and let them soak in: "The longer I live, the more I am certain that the great difference between the feeble and the powerful, the great and the insignificant, is energy, invincible determination, a purpose once fixed, and then death or victory."

Sir Fowell Buxton wrote this sentence 275 years ago. It is just as valid today as it was in his time. "Invincible determination" is the constant companion of successful people. It is the fuel that sustains them.

Walter Payton, nine-time Pro Bowl football player on the Chicago Bears, was asked to describe his greatest talent. Payton's answer provides a model for anyone who wants to succeed. "It's my ability to get back up on my feet," he replied. "Each time I got knocked down, I jumped right back up. Then I would get tackled again, and I jumped right back up. I knew that if I kept getting up, one of the next times I got knocked down I would jump back up *in the end zone.*"

When Johann Sebastian Bach was a boy, his older brother, believing that Johann's desire to become a composer was vain, destroyed his entire collection of musical scores. Johann was denied candles to work with at night, so he went out into the darkness the next evening and by moonlight wrote down from memory all the music that his brother had destroyed. Bach said, "I was determined not to let anyone keep me from my chosen destiny."

The will to persevere must be fed and nurtured on a daily basis. I love people who get up in the morning and say, "Good morning, Lord." Unfortunately, most people open their eyes, get out of bed, and say, "Good Lord, morning!"

Here are a few ways I nourish my will to persist:

- I make sure that every day I feed myself a constant meal of great motivational thoughts and sayings.
- I listen to motivational music. Over the years I've found it to be one of the most spirit-lifting powers on the planet. How could a person not get pumped up for a challenge when listening to Survivor's song, "The Eye of the Tiger"?
- At work I surround myself with one of the greatest teams an entrepreneur could dream of. I deliberately hire staff not just for their talent, but also for their can-do attitudes.

- I take quiet time for myself every day to restore, renew, and replenish my mind.
- I take pride in the empowerment that comes from my faith. Too many speakers are afraid they will repel an audience if they make references to religion or to God. But that's not me. I'm not ashamed of being a man of faith! Every man and woman who has this faith knows that it gives them the courage to persevere.
- I work out seriously every day. This helps me focus my mind and raise my energy level to try even harder.
- I never give up.

"Let me tell you the secret that has led me to my goal. My strength lies solely in my tenacity."

—*Louis Pasteur, French scientist*

The Most Powerful TV Sales Tool of Our Time

Let me give you another personal example of how perseverance can help you to victory, even when your chances of success seem like pie in the sky.

During the early 1990s the sales of my exercise videos on the Home Shopping Network were starting to slide. Times change, right? You have to change with them. I began checking out new ways to get my sales message across.

One tool that got my attention right away was a type of advertisement that was just beginning to show up on TV: the infomercial.

An infomercial is a 30-minute TV presentation that educates consumers about the benefits of a particular product, and that provides endorsements from satisfied customers who have used the product successfully. Not taken very seriously at first, infomercials were originally aired at weird hours, like from 2 AM to 6 AM. The thinking was that instead of signing off for the night and going black, as a lot of networks did in this era, they would run a string of these long-winded advertisements to fill in the dead time, and maybe make a few bucks out of it.

Then time passed and the network bosses began to look at the sales figures.

These half-hour sales jobs were not just filling up dead airspace. They were turning over tons of product and tons of money, even in the bloody middle of the night!

"Whoa!" network execs started to say. This is a really *powerful* way to sell your stuff! Soon infomercials were being aired on major channels throughout the day, and sometimes even during prime time.

In order to ride this new wave, I wanted to make an infomercial on a great new piece of exercise equipment I'd recently found called the Gazelle Free Style Glider. A type of elliptical trainer, the Gazelle was manufactured by Fitness Quest Inc., in Canton, Ohio. It was already being merchandised on several TV shopping channels across the country.

In 1996 I flew out to Canton and met with the CEO of Fitness Quest, Bob Schnabel.

It turned out that Bob was a fitness freak himself. He climbed mountains for a kick, and would one day dogsled across Alaska. He was also the guy responsible for promoting many successful shows including *Total Gym,* which was an "As Seen on TV" heavy hitter.

We sat down to lunch and came to a working arrangement right away. I would help redesign the Glider for television audiences. Then I'd follow up by producing a rock-'em, sock-'em infomercial to sell it.

Up 'til this time infomercials were modest productions featuring two or three people (usually including a Brit with a cockney accent for some reason) who sang the product's praises and gave hands-on demonstrations. Our version, we agreed, would raise the bar a few notches, and turn the infomercial into a form of entertainment. We'd film the commercial in a stylish gym using awesome music, a live audience, ridiculously sexy female demonstrators, and myself as the celebrity presenter—all new concepts for their time.

After we came to an agreement I set to work assembling a cast, studio, crew, and equipment, and right away I started getting a hit on this one. It was going to be *big*. Everybody else on the project had the same feeling. I couldn't wait to get at it!

"Getting ahead in a difficult profession requires avid faith in yourself. That is why some people with mediocre talent, but with great inner drive, go much further than people with vastly superior talent."

—*Sophia Loren, Italian film actress*

The Number of the Beast Gets My Number

It was October 31st, Halloween, just a few weeks before we were scheduled to shoot the first Gazelle Glider infomercial. That night I drove to a supper club with a friend in my brand-new NSX sports car, very sleek and low to the ground. I pulled into the parking lot and the attendant handed me a pink valet card. Printed on it in big bold figures was the number 666. This, in case you're snoozing, is the biblical Number of the Beast.

Now I'm not a particularly superstitious guy. But I got to tell you, people, this card really freaked me out!

It was Halloween night. The Number of the Beast had just been slipped into my hand. In a few weeks I was about to launch new career-making infomercials.

Was somebody out there trying to send me a message?

I handed the card back to the attendant and asked for a new one. My friend and I then went into the club, and I tried to forget the whole incident.

A few hours later I picked up the car and started driving home. The road I was on wound up and around what is probably the only hill in the entire state of Florida. Suddenly a vehicle from the ongoing traffic swerved into my lane.

I quickly whipped the car to the left to avoid a head-on collision. The sudden turn forced us off the side of the road and sent us spinning ass-over-elbow down a steep embankment. At the bottom of the hill the car collided with an enormous Florida swamp tree.

I freaked out. Then I blacked out.

"It is always too soon to quit."

—*Norman Vincent Peale, motivational speaker and author*

What's It Like Not to Have a Nose?

The next thing I remember is waking up in the ER with a concussion and a face I could have used to scare the crap out of people that Halloween night.

The end of my nose was cut in half. There was a deep, bloody cut down my lip exposing my teeth. My left cheek had a hole in it with a big sliced flap of meat and skin hanging off. The orbital bone over the corner of one of my eyes was broken.

When my kids saw me there in the emergency room they started to cry.

The hospital staff came in and went to work, cleaning the muck and dried blood off my face. They were about to start stitching up the wounds when I sat up, realized what was about to happen, and shouted out: "*Nobody* touches my face except a plastic surgeon!"

"Don't worry," one of the aides said. "We can handle it, Mr. Little. We do this kind of thing all the time."

"I don't care what you do all the time!" I roared. "I want a plastic surgeon!"

"But—"

"Plastic surgeon!"

Repetition, repetition, repetition.

A plastic surgeon was finally called in. They couldn't put me under anesthesia for the surgery because I had a concussion. So my sister Vicky, a nurse, stood by the bed and held my hand as they injected needle after needle into my nose, lips, cheek, and eye areas until I was numb enough to fix.

Five hours later the surgeon had more or less sewn my various features back together. By the end of the operation I had 200 stitches crisscrossing the face that in a few weeks was scheduled to be shown on an infomercial that would be seen by millions of Americans across the United States.

Not!

Fitness Quest was immediately informed of the car accident and was told that I'd been banged up pretty badly.

They asked to see pictures of my face. When the photos arrived in Canton, Bob Schnabel looked them over and got on the phone to me at once.

"Look, Tony," he said, "we love you. But you can't shoot an exercise video looking like this. We'll have to get someone to stand in for you this time."

I really needed this job to stay on top in TV sales. I really believed in the Gazelle. *Most* important, I knew that if I could get on the air and pitch this thing, it would take off like a rocket ship. But only if *I* sold it! It was my baby! I wanted it, I needed it, and I refused to quit!

Fine. Great. But, the truth of the matter was that my face was in shreds. Now was the time to see the handwriting on the wall and call it a day. Right? That's the prudent and reasonable thing to do in hopeless situations.

Not!

Because there's always a way. In this case, the way was belief in myself, belief in the product, and belief in the American people's empathy and understanding.

What Do Americans Believe In Most?

A day after I was released from the hospital, I jumped on a plane and flew to Canton to meet with Bob Schnabel.

I could tell right away that he was absolutely dead set against using me in the commercial. What the heck, I couldn't blame him. Who's going buy an exercise machine from the Phantom of the Opera? At least this was the common wisdom. But there's always a way.

"All due respects, Tony," he said. "You can't sell the Gazelle on TV looking like this. Heal up a bit and we'll see about using you on an info later on."

"You're missing the point, Bob!" I said.

"And that would be . . . ?"

"If you don't use me in this ad, we'll be missing the financial opportunity of a lifetime."

"Which is . . . ?"

"I've got an awesome story to tell now!" I pressed. "About turning bad into good. I think the American public will buy more Gazelles when they hear it."

"All right, tell me the story.""

"The American public loves tales of adversity to victory," I explained. "I'll go on the air and say to them, look, I shouldn't be here in front of you today. I was in a bad car accident just a few days ago. It tore up my face pretty badly, as you can see. But I'm not going to let this stop me. I don't go backward. I've learned to go forward in life no matter what happens to me. That's a major lesson that fitness has taught me. And it can teach you the same. So let me show you this amaaaaaaazing piece of exercise equipment that you're going to love, and that's going to make you feel better, look better, work better—my new Gazelle Free Style Glider."

I was pacing up and down as I spoke.

"I want to talk to people's sympathies, emotions, and beliefs, Bob. People love to hear how you came back from the brink and turned misfortune into victory. They love recovery stories. They want you to succeed. Because it gives them hope that *they* can succeed!"

Our discussion went back and forth along these lines for some time. Bob was getting intrigued with the idea, but he still didn't think I could sell the 250,000 Gazelles we needed to make money.

Finally, I sat down and pulled a chair up close to him.

"Here's the deal," I said. "If I make this infomercial and I sell less than 250,000 machines, I'll go out and buy you a new 1997 Porsche Carrera. Okay? If I *do* sell 250,000 machines, you'll come down to Florida and buy me the same car. Wanna shake on it?"

Like many great CEOs, Bob's a positive person with a little bit of the gambler in him. The idea tickled him. We were on.

I shot the infomercial live. In the first 30 seconds of the show I announced to the audience that by all rights I shouldn't be on this stage today. Because I'd just gotten out of the hospital from a terrible car accident. As you can see, I told them, my face is pretty messed up.

I then flashed visuals on the screen showing me backstage an hour before showtime having makeup applied. The photos showed my face before the makeup had disguised the lacerations and stitches. There was a big audience for the show and they responded sympathetically with applause and lots of "oh's" and "ah's." I then turned to the audience and said, "Look, it's not what happens to you in this life that matters. It's how you respond to it."

It was the first time I'd ever made this statement on TV. But it was definitely not the last. That slogan remained my theme in business and in life from that time on.

I then launched into my sales pitch for the Gazelle.

Not too long after this, Bob Schnabel, always true to his word, was on a jet down to Tampa Bay, Florida, to buy me a new white

1997 Porsche. The infomercial went on to gross $66 million. The last time I checked we'd sold more than seven million Gazelle Gliders around the world for over $1 billion.

Perseverance will always overcome.

Harry Jamieson, a hardware salesman famous for his persistence (he once made 125 sales calls on a prospect before the prospect put in an order), was asked how many calls he made on a potential customer before he threw in the towel. "Depends on which one of us dies first," Jamieson replied.

Tony's Seven Mighty Ways to Persist

1. Whatever you're trying to accomplish, always have hope. "I made 49 sales calls selling fancy stationery door to door," a cousin of mine told me years ago. "The 50th person I visited bought the stationery on the spot, with great pleasure, and this made all my previous efforts worth my time." I never forgot that lesson.
2. See your glass half full, not half empty. Okay, but full of what? Depends on the things you have inside you to fill it with.
3. Consider the feelings of others. Be generous with your time and help, even with the ungenerous. Remember the saying: "Kindness is loving people more than they deserve."
4. Focus your awareness completely on the problem at hand. Avoid distractions, daydreaming, diversions. Be totally in the present time when you do a job. Be there when you're there.
5. Don't change your plans too easily. Always have a strategy, and stick to it. Weak people wobble.
6. Consider every setback a step on your own personal, tailor-made ladder to the top of the heap. Visualize your own banner waving up there on the summit.

7. When things aren't going well, double your efforts. Then triple them. Then quadruple them. Never quit. Never quit. Never quit. Quitting is the only way you really lose!

Someone once mentioned to Thomas Edison the vast number of failures he'd experienced while attempting to build a reliable storage battery. "Approximately 50,000 failures," said this person. "That's a lot of failures before achieving any results." "Results?" Edison replied. "Why, I have gotten a lot of results. I know 50,000 things that won't work!"

10

Give It All You've Got!

"All things are possible until they are proved impossible, and even the impossible may only be so, as of now."

—*Pearl S. Buck, American author*

"You have to know, not only in your mind but also in your heart, 'I want this.'"

—*Sir David Michels, former Group Chief Executive, Hilton Hotels*

"You just can't beat the person who will never give up."

—*Babe Ruth, baseball great*

"Just don't give up trying to do what you want to do."

—*Ella Fitzgerald, singer*

"Never confuse a single defeat with a final defeat."

—*F. Scott Fitzgerald, American author*

Give It All You've Got!

How to Master Any Situation

Much of my career has been empowered by what I call "obvious secrets."

An obvious secret is a truism that nobody pays any attention to. It's a life-altering fact that everybody learns and then forgets.

For example, here's an "obvious secret" that has helped me achieve my goals better than anything I ever learned in school: If you're going to master the task before you, *you have to give it everything you've got.* Always. Everywhere. All the time. All the way.

Obvious?

Actually, the number of people I meet in the business community who ignore this super-important truth is staggering. "Trying" for so many people means making an effort twice or three times. Not ten times. Or a hundred.

Or a thousand.

Whatever it takes.

When Thomas Edison was working in his New Jersey laboratory to perfect the electric lightbulb, his attempts to come up with an efficient lighting filament failed *thousands of times* before he finally developed the modern incandescent bulb. *That's* giving it everything you've got.

When early film star Charlie Chaplin made a movie, he sometimes shot 500 takes of the same scene before he considered one take good enough to print.

In one sequence, for example, from an early silent comedy you can see Chaplin, acting as director and performer, staggering down a rickety flight of stairs in a bar. Not good enough. Next scene he tumbles down the stairs. Not good enough. Next scene he tumbles down the stairs and lands on a big fat man. Not good enough. Next scene he and the fat man tumble down the stairs together. Not good enough.

Take after take follows. Great scene after great scene—until, finally, the master is satisfied that he has tried his hardest and reached perfection.

Before I attend a meeting, I think of myself as a soldier going into battle. I'm on a mission. I *must* succeed. I review everything that's going to be on the table that day. I think about each person who's going to be sitting across from me—that person's personality, strengths, weaknesses, psychological agendas. I prepare mentally. I think positively. I start the day early with a workout so there's lots of oxygen going to my brain, and so all the fuzz is out of my head. I do everything I *possibly* can to be at peak performance, and to use all the weapons in my arsenal. It's better to have more ammunition than less, right?

When I was in high school, there was a halfback on our team who gained four or five yards every time he carried the ball. This fellow was short and not particularly fast or strong. Yet somehow he always seemed to bull his way through the opponents and knock them down, even the big ones. We were sitting together one day in the back of the school and I asked him what his secret was.

"Not much," he told me. And I never forgot his answer. "Each time I know the quarterback is going to give me the ball I just think to myself, 'If I don't make at least *three yards* this carry, they'll put me in jail for the rest of my life.' This way, every time I carry the ball I'm so determined no one can stop me."

"When I swing at the ball," baseball great Mickey Mantle once remarked, "I swing with everything I have—including my teeth."

When the "Please don't squeeze the Charmin™" TV ad was aired in 1978 featuring a naughty Mr. Whipple secretly fingering rolls of Charmin™ tissue on the supermarket shelves, the clip was heralded by critics as the most effective advertisement ever made. Versions of it went on to run for 21 years. At one point Mr. Whipple (played by Dick Wilson from the beloved TV show *Bewitched*) topped U.S. President Jimmy Carter as the most recognizable face in North America. That same year Procter & Gamble, manufacturers of

Charmin™, reported that Mr. Whipple was the third-best-known American male, behind ousted President Richard Nixon and evangelist Billy Graham. What most TV viewers *didn't* know was that it took the film crew over *700 takes* before the producers considered the ad ready for airtime.

Here are other examples I like of people who gave it all they had:

- Maya Angelou grew up sexually abused. Today she is one of America's most acknowledged poets.
- Onetime major league pitcher Jim Abbot was born without a right hand.
- Renaissance genius Leonardo da Vinci was dyslexic.
- Acclaimed actor Samuel L. Jackson suffered from a speech impediment. He worked on improving this flaw for many years because he had the will to succeed as an actor.
- Howard Schultz, chairman of Starbucks, was raised in a public housing project.
- President Andrew Jackson was an orphan.
- Steel baron Andrew Carnegie was so poor as a child he had to drop out of school in fourth grade and go to work as a laborer earning two cents an hour.

And here's one for the ages:

When he was seven years old he was the main financial support of his family. His mother died when he was nine. At 23 he declared bankruptcy. That same year he ran for state legislature and lost. At 26 he inherited a huge financial debt from his partner's death. A year later he had a nervous breakdown. At 29 he was defeated for house speaker. Two years later he lost a bid for elector. By the time he was 35 he'd run for Congress twice and lost both times. At 41 he experienced the death of his four-year-old son, and his wife began showing signs of insanity. At 45 he lost the vice presidential nomination. At 49 he ran for Senate and lost again.

You know who I'm talking about: Abraham Lincoln.

The only barriers we face in life are the barriers we build in our minds. The only impossible obstacles are the ones we place in our own path. The only "no's" that are unchangeable are the "no's" we whisper in our own ear.

There is always, always, always a way.

"Courage means to keep working a relationship, to continue seeking solutions to difficult problems, to stay focused during stressful periods."

—*Denis Waitley, motivational business writer*

Everything You've Got!

Several months after I got out of the hospital from my accident with the school bus I landed a job working for United Parcel Service. When you start with this giant organization, they put you to work on the lowest rung of their very tall totem pole. That would be unloading mail trucks, sorting out the packages, and loading them onto a conveyor belt.

It was backbreaking work; and after the accident I didn't have a very good back. Nevertheless, I decided from the first day that if I was going to do this job I'd be the *fastest truck unloader* in UPS history! Heck, I'd make loading and unloading into a workout. It was a chance to rebuild my body and get my muscles strong again. I'd give it everything I had!

The first day on the job working with a couple of other guys, I unloaded the truck and got the packages onto the conveyor belt so fast that every 10 or 15 minutes they had to shut the belt down to catch up. After an hour or so of turning it off and on, my supervisor yelled into the truck, "Little! Slow it down, slow it down! You're going so fast you're messing up the belt!"

The guys I was working with hated me, of course, because I was making them look lazy. But after a while they started speeding up, too, to prove they had cojones. If the *Guinness Book of World Records* had ever recorded the fastest truck unloading team in UPS history, we would have held all the records.

I worked so hard that after a couple of weeks they promoted me to truck washer. My job now was to wash and vacuum 45 UPS trucks a day on the huge UPS lot.

That's a lot of trucks! And the UPS drivers didn't make my job any easier. Whenever they drove their vehicles to the UPS office early in the morning to be washed, instead of parking them in their assigned spaces they'd leave them all over the lot. Most of my morning was spent looking for my assigned trucks and driving them into the washing area. The cleaning part was easy.

After a couple of days of wasting time this way I decided to make some changes.

Next morning I got up an hour early, showed up to the lot, and as the drivers pulled in I played policeman, directing each truck into its assigned space. This way I didn't waste the morning searching for the trucks, and I could finish up washing my quota of vehicles by 10 or 11 o'clock. Then I'd take the rest of the time off and sleep!

Moral: Be creative. Jump over the status quo. Work as hard as you can. Don't worry what others think of you. And work at it, work at it, work at it, until you're *totally* satisfied with the results.

"In the trying," goes the saying, "is the succeeding."

"I always remember an epitaph which is in a cemetery in Tombstone, Arizona. It says, 'Here lies Jack Williams. He done his damnedest.' I think this is the greatest epitaph a man can have."

—*Harry Truman, U.S. president*

The Cosmetics Warrior

Mary Kathlyn Wagner was born in Texas in 1918. Her father was crippled with tuberculosis, and as a teenager Mary Kay, as she was called by her friends, was forced to nurse her dad *and* run the family household while her mother worked.

A straight-A student in high school, Mary Kay was too poor to afford college. She married a local boy, had three children in seven years, and stayed home throughout the 1930s in Depression-era Texas minding the kids and keeping house.

When her husband returned home from World War II, he demanded a divorce. He then disappeared from the scene, and Mary Kay was left penniless, the sole support of her three young children. "I had developed a sense of worth for my abilities as a wife and mother," she wrote in her autobiography, "and yet on that day I felt like a complete and total failure."

So far not exactly the stuff of sales stardom and international success.

In 1963, while beginning to climb the ladder of success at a company called World Gift, Mary Kay ran into the most common antiwoman barrier in the business world: the glass ceiling. A lower-ranking male colleague was given a promotion that she'd been promised. "I was constantly being told, 'Oh, Mary Kay, you're thinking female.' And inevitably, no matter how hard I tried, no matter how well I did in my job, I still found myself reaching the golden door only to find it marked Men Only."

Disgusted with the system, anxious to do her own business thing, Mary Kay quit—and immediately fell into a deep depression.

But she would not give up. In the depths of despair, she started compiling a list of both her special abilities and the obstacles she needed to overcome to be a success. While making this list, almost as an afterthought, she drew up a definition of her "dream company"—a women-based organization staffed by a fleet of trained saleswomen who sold high-quality skin-care products to a waiting female world.

Then came the idea: why not *do* it? Why not start the company? With all her heart and soul!

To succeed, Mary Kay first had to go head-to-head with her Goliath-sized competitor, Avon Products, Inc.

This was fine with her. She had a plan.

Noting that the house-to-house "Avon calling!" sales approach was losing popularity, she redesigned the skin-care door-to-door trade by creating a task force of female "cosmetics consultants."

These relatively well-trained saleswomen organized parties of five or six housewives at one of the women's homes. The Mary Kay consultant would then offer beauty advice to participants, demonstrate the best way to apply face creams, perform makeovers, and, of course, sell the Mary Kay line of cosmetics. After they had learned the ropes and started making money for the company, consultants could then recruit other consultants. Very soon the ranks of Mary Kay employees began to swell.

The rest is history. In 1964 Mary Kay's company had 200 employees. Eight years later it had several thousand, and her company had become one of the nation's largest employers of women in an era when the glass ceiling still hung low.

So there you have it.

For Edison, for Chaplin, for the creators of the Charmin™ commercial, for never-say-die Mary Kay, and for every dedicated businessperson, "trying" does not mean just trying hard. It means trying with every inch of yourself, with every last bit of stamina, will, and desire you possess until you get it right.

"I want to be remembered as the ball player who gave all he had to give."

—*Roberto Clemente, baseball player*

"Anna Nicole Smith Loses Weight . . . Trainer!"

In 2003 I took on what most of the male world would consider a mouthwatering assignment.

The gig: Star in a weekly TV reality show on the E! Channel.

The theme of the show: Use my fitness skills to transform TV starlet Anna Nicole Smith's overweight body back to the curvy shape it displayed when she posed for her famous *Playboy* centerfold.

Hear me, people. This was *no easy job*!

I started working with Anna just a few years before her tragic drug-induced death. At the time she was already carrying more than 40 extra pounds on her five feet 11 inch frame. At one point in her career she would balloon up to 230 pounds.

From the start her attitude sucked. As one newspaper article reported, "Tony may be the king of discipline. But Anna's love of food is just as strong as he is. It's going to be a real tug-of-war!"

As the E! cameras rolled in Anna's Los Angeles home, I tried to coax her out of her junk food habit and onto the exercise machines. Her response was always the same. She'd gaze up at me and say, "Tony, I just don't feel like working out today—give me a big hug instead."

When I tried to drag her out of her king-size bed at one o'clock in the afternoon and get her on the Gazelle, she'd coo, "Come out with us to McDonald's, Tony. I don't need to work out today." As one newspaper article reported, "The irresistible force, Tony Little, has met the immovable object, Anna Nicole Smith. The meeting proved once again that for people who want to sabotage their careers, couch potatoship wins every time!"

After about a week of these games I realized that Anna Nicole Smith was a card-carrying member of the "no pain, no sprain" exercise-phobic crowd, and that she was simply not going to change. You have to *want* to change to get the benefits of change.

"I take rejection as someone blowing a bugle in my ear to wake me up and get going, rather than retreat."

—*Sylvester Stallone, actor*

It is never easy for me to walk away from a challenge. But when the person you're trying to help has no interest in getting better or making an effort, there's no choice. I called it quits and walked out, making big news in all the tabloids. One headline read: "Anna Loses 200 lbs—Her Trainer!"

The saddest part of the whole affair is that I know in my heart today that Anna's life would not have ended so tragically if she had only found that spark of resolve inside herself to work hard, stick to it, and give it everything she had.

"Boys, there ain't no free lunches in this country. And don't go spending your whole life commiserating that you got the raw deals. You've got to say, 'I think that if I keep working at this and want it bad enough I can have it.' It's called perseverance."

—*Lee Iacocca, business author and former CEO of Chrysler Motors*

Harnessing the Power of Purpose

Napoleon Hill talks a lot about "Definiteness of Purpose."

According to this legendary motivator, 98 out of every 100 people fail to develop Definiteness of Purpose in their business lives and in their personal lives as well.

This purpose should not just be a wish or hope, Hill insists. It should be "a burning desire." Even an *obsessional* desire. One you're willing to pay any price to achieve.

"The moment you choose your Definite Major Purpose in life," writes Hill, "you will observe a strange circumstance consisting in the fact that ways and means of attaining that purpose will begin immediately to reveal themselves to you. Opportunities you had not expected will be placed in your way. The cooperation of others will become available to you, and friends will appear as if by a stroke of magic."

Hill adds this important warning: "This may seem, to the uninitiated, a fantastic promise. But not so to the man who has done away with indecision and has chosen a definite goal in life."

You've heard of the famous samurai soldiers of Japan. These elite warriors conducted their affairs on and off the battlefield based on a simple and unchanging principle: Never give up. *Ever.*

If a samurai was in battle and his sword was knocked away, he fought with his hands. If his hands were cut off, he fought with his feet. If he was knocked to the ground, he fought lying on his back. He never gave up and he never gave in. He always gave 100 percent. This made him the most successful warrior the world has ever known.

Think of the martial arts. Ultimate fighting. A battler goes at his opponent with punches, head butts, roundhouse kicks, sweeps, take-down moves, karate blows, headlocks. Everything he's got.

This is how motivated salespersons think, too. Their weapons: enthusiasm, energy, technique. Good salespersons are informative, positive, polite, up-to-date. They have all the facts and figures you request at the ready. They demonstrate hands-on how their product works. If possible, they let you try it out. They formulate the answers to your questions before you ask them. They surprise you. They delight you. They make you laugh. They make you feel good. They make you *feel*. They lower your defense mechanisms slowly but surely, moving in for the close. Everything they've got.

Build that super effort, never say die, and the rewards will come to you almost automatically. I don't know how it works exactly, or why, but it does. You do your part. Fate and the world out there do the rest.

But don't believe me. Just try it.

Tony's Takeaways

- Giving it everything you have means just that and nothing less—*everything* you have!
- If you think you've reached your limits, you haven't.
- Limits are thoughts that arise in your head. Stop thinking them and they'll stop getting in your way.

- If you can't give 100 percent, then do the next best thing—give 90 percent. That will usually do the trick. And if not 90 percent, then, well, 80 percent. Never less than that, though.
- Supreme effort will almost always get the results you wish. This is not a mystical idea. It's a practical idea. But the effort *has* to be supreme.

11

Tell a Tale,
Make a Sale

"A good story is a story which is not too long and which gives the reader the feeling he has undergone a memorable experience."

—Kathleen Kenison, writer and editor

"Tell people a good tale and it's the same as giving them a present or inviting them to dinner. It makes people like you. They're interested in you. They want to know you now, and to become your friend. A good story is a great mind-changer and social device."

—Willa MacDonald, Internet blogger

"Some of my most successful ads started with a story. The story very often has very little to do with the product you're selling, or the service you're offering. But—people love stories. Because when they were very young they were read stories. That's how they communicated and understood the world."

—Joe Sugarman, copywriter and mail-order guru

"If you have anything to say, anything you feel nobody has ever said before, you have got to feel it so desperately that you will find some way to say it that nobody has ever found before, so that the thing you have to say and the way of saying it blend as one matter—as indissolubly as if they were conceived together."

—F. Scott Fitzgerald, American writer

Tell a Tale, Make a Sale

Do You Mind If I Grab Your Mind?

Have you noticed throughout these chapters that I've consistently used dramatic and sometimes sensational incidents from my own life to hook your attention? And how, as I tell stories about transforming my own hard times into the raw materials of success, I'm selling myself and my products as well?

I'm being brutally honest here, folks, because I want you to absorb what I'm going to tell you in the next few pages.

Storytelling, in many experts' estimation, is the *most effective moneymaking technique in the world.*

Why? Because a good story induces a kind of hypnotic trance in people's thought patterns. It "fascinates," to use the vocabulary of nineteenth-century hypnotists. A compelling narrative short-circuits people's defense mechanisms and speaks directly to their instincts and desires. It keeps them turned on, tuned in, and, from a selling point of view, wide open to suggestion. If a story is told well, and if it reflects a listener's fears, hopes, and dreams, it persuades them to trust you, to join your team, and to purchase your product.

"If history were taught in the form of stories, it would never be forgotten."

—*Rudyard Kipling, British author*

Of course, for my part, stories of adversity to victory are the best of stories. They show you how to succeed in all life's circumstances, and how the power of the human spirit can prevail in this very short time we have here on the planet Earth. What more could you ask from a sales technique?

You're Under My Spell!

I've told my adversity-to-victory tale hundreds of times, and it never fails to hold an audience's attention. When they hear this story, listeners see themselves in the situations I describe, and this brings back memories of their own losses and recoveries. They listen to the ups and downs, identify with the struggles, and are inspired to believe that they, too, can overcome the hardships that are robbing them of happiness.

In *Hypnotic Writing*, Joe Vitale describes many of the hidden factors in human communication that forge our opinions and stimulate us to buy. "Hypnotic writing," Vitale states plainly, "is intentionally using words to guide people into a focused mental state where they are inclined to buy your product or service."

Vitale describes a series of computer studies carried out several years ago at three British universities. The subject of these studies was the power of human words, and specifically the power of words used by famed English mystery writer Agatha Christie.

According to university research—the study was called the Agatha Project—Christie's deceptively simple prose produces measurable chemical changes in a reader's nervous system, all of a positive kind. The author's words, computer analyses reveal, are arranged in such stimulating patterns, and are chosen with such emotional precision, that they trigger mood-enhancing serotonin and endorphins inside a reader's brain. These, as you know, are the same feel-good substances that are released when we exercise and work out.

Vitale concludes that the great mystery writer's words and phrases cast a mesmerizing spell on the mind, and excite the pleasure-inducing side of the brain. He then makes the natural segue from words alone into the power of storytelling per se, promising readers that if they present their narratives in a convincing way to a listening public they will have this public eating from their hands. "This," he tells us, "is a hypnotic state of focused attention where people are riveted to your messages and are more inclined to do what you ask—such as buy from you."

Such is the power of story.

"Be amusing: never tell unkind stories; above all, never tell long ones."

—*Benjamin Disraeli, British prime minister*

Sales Lessons from Old-Time Musclemen

In my teenage years as a bodybuilder I read countless sales stories from famous workout gurus like Charles Atlas and Jack LaLanne. Addressing 12- to 18-year-old male readers like myself, these fitness pioneers sold millions of mail-order bodybuilding courses by weaving tales—who knows if they were true?—of their own physical transformation from a "97-pound weakling" (to quote Charles Atlas's iconic line) into powerfully built, mentally positive, and socially self-assured men of the world.

Advertisements showing Atlas's bronzed body appeared on the back of comic books, in newspapers, in men's magazines, and sometimes even on highway billboards. They were inevitably accompanied by his famous slogan, "You too can have a body like mine!"

His sales pitch always featured a version of the same plot. It went something like this.

A young man skinny enough to have just escaped from a concentration camp (presumably once Atlas himself) is strolling along the beach with his beautiful blonde girlfriend. A muscle-bound bully comes along, kicks sand in the young man's face, knocks him down, tells him his "ribs are showing," calls him a "97-pound weakling," and walks away laughing with the weakling's girlfriend clinging to his arm. The other beautiful people on the beach lying under their striped umbrellas laugh along with him.

What does the weakling do?

He sends for Charles Atlas's free introductory bodybuilding booklet.

He reads the brochure, buys the course, learns Atlas's secret system for building muscles (known famously as "dynamic tension"), and quickly begins sprouting gigantic arms and legs. A few months later he goes back to the beach looking like the Incredible Hulk, beats up the bully, and gets back his girl. The sales power of Atlas's advertisements is still legendary in advertising circles.

Another strongman who achieved fantastic success by telling a rags-to-riches yarn was Jack LaLanne.

This remarkable athlete is famous for his almost supernatural physical feats. He once swam the entire length of the Golden Gate Bridge underwater with 140 pounds of equipment strapped to his back. Another time he towed 10 boats at once carrying 77 people for a mile across the San Francisco Bay. At age 94 LaLanne was still lifting weights and working out every morning for two hours. A popular guest on interview shows, he often remarks that "I can't afford to die. It will ruin my image."

LaLanne told his Horatio Alger story to countless strongman wannabes like myself, describing how as a poor boy growing up in California he was weak, short, nervous, undernourished, antisocial, and addicted to sugar and junk food.

All this changed when he turned 15 and attended a lecture promoting exercise and diet. From that day on he began eating right, thinking positively, exercising daily, and beefing up. Before long he was a model specimen.

LaLanne eventually opened a series of 200 fitness spas across the United States—they were among the country's first health clubs—and went on to earn hundreds of millions of dollars selling juicers, vitamins, kitchen equipment, and fitness videos, all the time using the story of his teenage transformation from "pee-wee to powerful" to promote his line of goods. It was no coincidence, perhaps, that years later LaLanne would win a prize that was actually called the Horatio Alger Award from the Association of Distinguished Americans. His life has been a rags-to-riches story on steroids.

I'm proud to say, by the way, that I know Jack personally, and that he truly is the father of fitness in America. I've told him many times that while he's able to tow armadas of boats across the San Francisco

Bay, if I tried hauling just one rowboat I'd drown in five minutes. He and his wife Elaine always laugh when they hear my description.

The power of story again.

How to Create the Desire to Consume in a Sentence

Are you seeing a trend here, folks? Entertaining story lines sell, and they can help you sell, too. Use them in office copy, when entertaining clients, and especially when making a sales presentation.

Look, for example, at the list of slogans that follows. It contains some of the most famous corporate ad lines of our time, each designed to weave a spell of fear, need, success, and desire in the reader—and sometimes a combination of all four.

- **Need:** A day without orange juice is a like day without sunshine. (Florida Citrus Commission)
- **Fear, need, success:** When it absolutely, positively has to be there overnight. (Federal Express)
- **Fear:** There are a million and one excuses for not wearing a safety belt. Some are real killers. (American Safety Council)
- **Desire:** A diamond is forever. (De Beers Consolidated Mines)
- **Fear:** Don't leave home without it. (American Express credit card)
- **Desire:** Hey! You never know! (Lotto)
- **Need and desire:** Where's the beef? (Wendy's)
- **Need and desire:** The power to be your best. (Apple computers)
- **Desire:** Promise her anything, but give her Arpege. (Arpege perfumes)
- **Need and success:** Our repairmen are the loneliest guys in town. (Maytag Appliances)
- **Need, success, desire:** You can do it! (Tony Little in a Geico ad)

What makes these slogans so memorable and persuasive?

First, they pose a problem in the listener's mind. Usually it's a common problem that many people worry about. Do I have enough money? Do people like me? Is my house clean enough? Do I smell?

Am I getting sick? Am I falling behind the competition? Then they provide, or more often imply, an attractive and exciting solution.

Each of these slogans is also a complete mini-story with a beginning chapter, middle chapter, and end. These chapters are mostly implied, but it's amazing how much intrigue and adventure can be packed into a few choice words. The best commercial slogans suggest plots you might use for a short story or even a novel.

Tonight when you watch TV, pay special attention to the advertisements. Notice how they play on conflict-struggle-resolution situations, a motif you'll find at the heart of any good tale.

One series of TV commercials that's aired a lot these days, the Geico insurance ads, is particularly close to my heart. (I was once featured on a Geico ad myself yelling, "You can do it!") Especially entertaining is the Geico Gecko, a sales story that has all the elements of mock tragedy and laugh-out-loud comedy. The main character in these segments is an up-from-the-bottom (of the swamp) little green guy who's been stepped on and neglected all his life, like most geckos. Hey, it's not easy being green!

But this humble and kindly little reptile is special. Through his own hard work, and by applying his keen sense of people's insurance needs, he has risen to the very top of the corporate ladder. Several commercials show him talking shop with the company's CEO. A printed ad calls him "arguably the world's most successful business gecko." Another announces that he's a close friend of Warren Buffett ("Warren Buffett and the Gecko. They go together like pie and chips."). It's a classic adversity-to-victory tale in miniature, with an underlying "nice guys do finish first" theme that goes right to the heart.

See what I mean? People are using stories all the time to sell you things, even when you don't know it.

Think Story in Everything You Do

It's important to keep in mind that the narrative you use to arouse buying interest in customers does *not* have to be *War and Peace*. A story can take a lot of forms. It can be an anecdote, a case study, an endorsement. It can be a comment, a testimonial, a Q&A exchange, even a joke. It can be shoehorned into practically any presentation or sales routine or report or sales letter. You can make a set of instructions into a story. Or a pep talk, a sales brochure, a piece of documentation, a white paper, a staff review, a job interview.

Here are some story techniques I use when I'm pitching a project or idea.

- **The big bad wolf is lurking.** I dramatize sales presentations by presenting some type of menace or conflict. I ask people: If you knew that the meat you're feeding your family contains 107 different toxic chemicals, would you consider switching to an additive-free meat like my bison burgers? If you knew your pillow was sabotaging your sleep *and* your posture, would you be interested in buying a better pillow? If your sandals are giving you blisters and falling off your feet, would you like to hear about sandals that fit better, and that exercise your legs when you walk? As the saying goes among film writers, "No conflict, no story, no film."
- **Learn storytelling from newspaper headlines.** Scan your newspaper. See how the better headlines tell a story in a nutshell—a mystery, a scandal, a triumph, a painful moment, an unresolved conflict. In the *New York Times* this morning I found the following lead tags:
  - Women Fighting Alongside Men in Afghanistan, and Fitting In.
  - With Dad Laid Off, Finding Ways to Hold On.
  - Fox Business Needs a Lift. Could It Be Don Imus?
  - Meeting of Many Minds (and Bodies).
  - Brad Pitt Pulls Them In for a "Glorious Weekend."

    They make you want to know more, right? They keep you reading. Stories enthrall.
- **Use your own rags-to-riches tale.** Whenever I can, I use rags to riches in my own sales copy. Everybody likes to read tales of upward mobility and beating the system. Describe how you or

your company fought its way to prominence by gaining market share from three large competitors. Tell how you started work at your company fixing water fountains, and today you're the floor manager. Explain how one of your employees has recently come back to work after struggling with a life-threatening disease. Human stories create human interest.

- **Apply the power of testimonials.** A happy customer describing how much she loves a product and how much it improved her life is one of the true powers in the selling universe. Here is a testimonial from the "Stories" section of my web site. Notice how well this person's tale communicates real interest and feeling. "I'm writing this letter to let you know what a difference your programs have made in my life. When I started I weighed 245 pounds, and had a 42-inch waist. In just 10 weeks I weighed 190 pounds, and had a 36-inch waist! I can't believe I lost all that weight by doing the exercises you recommended five to seven minutes a day. I looked at pictures of my old self, and asked my friends how could they let me look like that! I thought I was happy at the time I was overweight, but I was wrong. I am thrilled with my new looks!"

- **Get personal.** When I want to gain a customer's or a colleague's trust, I sometimes relate an interesting or dramatic event from my own past. This story doesn't necessarily reveal my intimate secrets. It does, however, let clients know that I'm friendly, open, and human.

- **Take a lead from film and TV writers.** Start out right away with a story that grabs people's attention. Film and TV shows use this device all the time. It's called a teaser. When I was running my spa-cleaning company, I'd drum up business by approaching spa owners and, first thing out of my mouth, asking them if they knew there were approximately a billion staph germs living in the average hot tub. I'd tell them that many dangerous bacterial germs like cryptosporidum are not killed by hot water. I'd scare them with the fact that there are more than 100 lawsuits filed every year in the United States against gyms by members who claim they were infected while working out. These provocative teasers alarmed the gym owners and immediately got them interested in my cleaning services, which, by the way, they badly needed!

- **Keep it in the family.** When you have a successful sales story to tell, a lot of people in the office will want to hear it. Tell your coworkers the good news in e-letters, on your web site, in annual reports, in newsletters, and during training sessions. Some business execs I know hold "fireside chats" with staff members to tell motivational stories and build team spirit. Success stories raise endorphins and create feelings of group solidarity. Use them.

- **Mix your media.** Tell your story in film, on TV, in sales letters, on the Web. Tell it by e-mail, on Twitter, in white papers, in webinars, in case studies, in photographs, in advertisements, in training videos, in printed material. Tell it verbally at lectures, clubs, dinners, conventions, business meetings, colleges, schools, conferences, training sessions, and any other place where an intriguing story will help get your foot in the door.

- **Ask others to tell their stories.** Encourage colleagues and customers to tell their stories. Some companies (like mine) feature a "share your story" option on their web sites. Others feature story sections in e-letters and newsletters. People like to hear positive, uplifting stories that elevate their moods and confirm their belief systems. Uplifting stories told with purpose and enthusiasm can change the world. Start telling them now.

Tony's Seven Tips on Story

1. When telling a sales story, it's a lot better to appeal to people's emotions, desire, and curiosity than to their reason or intellect. Speaking to the mind gets them interested, but speaking to their heart makes the sale.

2. When you tell your tale, speak quickly, enunciate well, and make important points with dramatic emphasis.

3. Believe in what you're saying. Clients and customers will know when you're faking it.
4. Keep people interested by promising them that in the next few minutes you're going to tell them something *very* important.
5. When you tell a selling story, always try to put at least one fascinating fact into it.
6. If you tell a story, 30 to 60 seconds is about the right length of time to spin it out. Too many characters, too complex a plot, and you're guaranteed to make them snooze.
7. Any story is better when leavened with humor.

Tony's Three Guaranteed Storytelling Techniques

1. **Present a mystery, then unravel it in stages.** What is the mysterious force that keeps interfering with our sales plan? What caused such a powerful franchise to lose money? How could the marketing information our researchers came up with be so off the mark? Why isn't your treadmill helping you lose weight? Present the puzzle, then provide answers piece by piece.
2. **Present a situation of jeopardy for listeners, then resolve it.** A critic once remarked that the essence of any drama is as follows: In the first act you drive your heroine up a tree. In the second act you throw stones at her. In the third act you get her down. In the first part of your presentation, establish the trouble point: Our cherry crop has a serious blight this year. Our accountants can't figure out where the money is leaking. Then develop the problem, adding details. Finally, suggest or brainstorm a solution.
3. **Use a story to identify a problem listeners are personally experiencing, and show them how to overcome it.** Are people in your office searching for the best credit insurance? Tell

(continued)

them where to find it. Are your listeners worried about the recent firing of several managers? Explain the positive side of the situation. You, I, and everyone else listen to what is being told to us, and sold to us, with the same basic question: What's in it for me? Profit? Promotion? Enhanced reputation? A vacation? Identify the personal problems of the people you're talking to, then give them the remedies.

My mom and dad.

My mom, dad, brother, and sisters. I am in the bib overalls. 1959.

This is the only time you will ever see me with a bow tie. I don't know my age here, but obviously young and innocent.

ATTENDANCE

DAYS ABSENT.......	1	0
TIMES TARDY.......		

TO THE PARENT—OUR PARTNER:

May we work together in a common interest—that of our children.

Through this progress report we present you with a picture of your child's social habits and capabilities as well as his progress in the subject matter areas.

We wish to call to your attention the fact that no two individuals are alike in all respects, and we must be conscious of this at all times. Please do not, therefore, compare your child with other children but measure him according to his ability.

If your child does things successfully, commend him. If his progress report indicates that he needs additional help, do not reprimand him but better, come to the school for a conference where his problems may be discussed with the one who knows most about his social and his work habits—the teacher.

Many hours are devoted to knowing your child better during the time he spends in our schools. And we want you to know, that no opportunity is ever lost in the development of your child's personality along happy and wholesome channels.

With your interest, your cooperation, and your understanding, such goals as outlined above are easily attainable.

———— SIGNATURES ————

1st_____

2nd_____

FATHER - MOTHER - CHILD - TEACHER

LET'S WORK TOGETHER

Copyright—Acadia Press, Taylor, Penna.

Kindergarten Report of Progress

19**61**   19**62**

PUPIL'S NAME Tony Little

SCHOOL Stamm

TEACHER Miss Thelma Keiser

Anthony

(*has help with zipper)

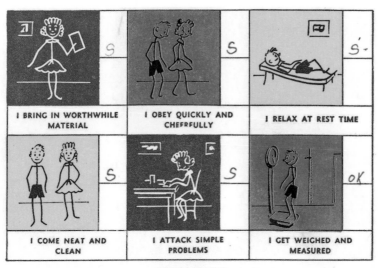

I BRING IN WORTHWHILE MATERIAL — S	I OBEY QUICKLY AND CHEERFULLY — S	I RELAX AT REST TIME — S-
I COME NEAT AND CLEAN — S	I ATTACK SIMPLE PROBLEMS — S	I GET WEIGHED AND MEASURED — OK

COMMENTS

1st Period Anthony "demands" my attention - quite often is quite---- -persistent! (altho' it takes a little while to under-stand him. I am enjoying having him, in the class.

2nd Period Tony is our "scientist" - having brought quite a lot to show-- one; the "Volcano"- lava from New Mexico" (which his Gran-mother brought).

Promoted.

(Thank You - so much for the very nice Perfume!) I've enjoyed it!

EXPLANATION OF MARKS

S--SATISFACTORY   I--IMPROVEMENT SHOWN

N--NEED FOR IMPROVEMENT

Eighteen years old, at my grandparents' house in Inverness, Florida.

I finally won Mr. Florida and I wasn't going to let go of my trophy – not bad legs! 1981.

At the height of my career shape – before my bus accident. 1982.

Original depressed and fat photo – after my bus accident. No work! No job! No exercise! 1983.

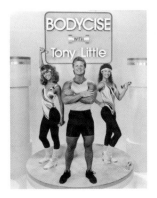

My first exercise show on Cable TV. 1985.

From my first Personal Trainer photo shoot. 1993.

At Universal Studios with Clyde from my first kids' exercise video. 1994.

A promotional shot. Some of the shots from this session were later used for the great *Muscle & Fitness* magazine. 1995.

In my St. Petersburg, Florida office. I'm all business now – or at least I think I look it. 1995.

The calmer side of me, a casual shot at my office. 1996.

My NSX sports car from Halloween night – after getting the valet parking ticket 666. 1996.

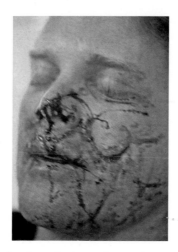

Me at the hospital after being cleaned up and 200 stitches later. 1996.

Proud Dad with Trent and Tara – the loves of my life – when they were 3- and 4-years old, respectively.

With my kids outside at our house. They have always been my best friends. Around 1996.

WANTED

TONY LITTLE
America's Personal Trainer™

The photo I mocked up for my P.R. kits in the late 90s. Thankfully, I wasn't wanted for my Juvenile Delinquent days, but for positive jobs.

Wanted to show I had hair – and a custom Pro Sport Harley. 1997.

Me and my life size stand up (LOL), displayed in stores in the USA. 2001.

Says it all! You are what you eat! A shot from my book *One on One*. 2003.

At HSN, with my makeup artist, who has to work on me for hours to make me look good. 2007.

My ultimate gift to myself – Porsche Turbo. My first real super car. Darn that felt good. 2007.

Me with a big tool and my 1967 GTO. My first car was a 1967 GTO, pearl green with obnoxious white header pipes. 2008.

My birthday photo shoot, telling people "you can't hold me down." Every birthday I hold a 1- or 2-day shoot just to get a crazy or dramatic shot for marketing and promotion.

Tara and Trent – a little bigger, a little smarter, and still my best friends. Christmas 2008.

"There's always a way" photo shoot with Jorge Alvarez. Another off-the-wall P.R. and marketing shot. 2009.

My wife, Melissa, and me – two regular fitness people. 2009.

Love at first sight – she proposed to me. She sold me, then closed me. Paradise Island, Bahamas, 2009.

My mime at my wedding at the One and Only Ocean Club in the Bahamas. I also had contortionists, fire dancers, etc. I hate boring weddings. 2009.

My dream comes true. Ernst and Young Entrepreneur of the Year Award – Florida. Category of Media, Marketing, and Entertainment. 2009.

12

Be Smart: Keep It Simple

"The more simply and plainly an idea is presented, the more under-standable it is—and therefore the more credible it will be."

—*Dr. Frank Luntz, political and advertising pollster*

"Live simply that others might simply live."

—*Elizabeth Seaton, educator, founder of Catholic school system in America*

"Any intelligent fool can make things bigger, more complex, and more violent. It takes a touch of genius—and a lot of courage—to move in the opposite direction."

—*E. F. Schumacker, German economist and author of Small Is Beautiful*

"And all the loveliest things there be
Come simply, so, it seems to me."

—*Edna St. Vincent Millay, American poet*

Be Smart: Keep It Simple

It Pays to Be Simple

The great physicist Albert Einstein was once delivering a speech at Princeton University before a high-achieving group of young physicists.

"The laws of physics should be simple," Einstein decreed.

A student in the audience piped up, "But what if they are not so simple?"

"Then I would not be interested in them," Einstein replied.

That's the kind of advice I like to give. It's the kind I like to get, too.

I'm basically a simple guy. No BS. When I sell, I concentrate on a few important points. I don't like to balance too many balls in the air. I think too many balls are a distraction. I keep my sentences crisp, uncomplicated, and short. "Nothing is lacking," some guy from the Renaissance once said, "but nothing is superfluous."

That's a great way of telling you to keep it simple.

"Avoid words that might force someone to reach for the dictionary," advises political pollster Dr. Frank Luntz in his amazing book, *Words That Work* (Hyperion, 2006). "Because most Americans won't. They'll just placidly let your real meaning sail over their heads or, even worse, misunderstand you. You can argue all you want about the dumbing down of America, but unless you speak the language of your intended audience, you won't be heard by the people you want to reach."

President Calvin Coolidge was both sparing in his words and famous for delivering brief, terse speeches. One day a close friend tried to pin him down. "I'll bet you I can rouse you out of your silence and make you say at least three words," the friend challenged.

"You lose," was Coolidge's reply.

When O. J. Simpson's lawyer, Robert Shapiro, needed to dispute the prosecution's DNA findings, he called in an expert forensic witness named Dr. Henry Lee. Dr. Lee was asked about the authenticity of the DNA of Nicole Simpson that had been discovered on O. J. Simpson's clothes. He answered in two simple words that blew open the case and changed the course of the trial: "Something wrong." Short, sweet, definitely definitive. (And, of course, there was always defense attorney Johnnie Cochran's famous one-liner about the bloody glove: "If it doesn't fit, you must acquit.")

Americans love to keep it simple. We prefer abbreviations, acronyms, headlines, and sound bites to lengthy tomes. We believe a simple message is a more understandable message. Advertisers play to this preference with shorties like "I'm lovin' it," "Finger lickin' good," "Intel inside," and "It's the real thing." We like to keep it tight in our e-mail and text messages, too. I mean, how much more can you water down a message than the one I recently got from one of my kids: "hey, yr home. B in touch, ok. C U at 8."

Sometimes less is more.

"Making the simple complicated is commonplace; making the complicated simple, awesomely simple, that's creativity."

—*Charles Mingus, jazz musician*

Joe Gold was a pioneer in the bodybuilding profession and founder of the famous Joe Gold gym. He was known to be a careful, neat, and together kind of guy. When young bodybuilders asked for his advice, he told them to take the simple route in life and in sports.

"To keep it simple," Joe once said, "you run your gym like you run your house. Keep it clean and in good running order. No jerks allowed, members pay on time, and if they give you any crap, throw them out. There's peace where there's order."

Yeah, baby! Peace where there's order. Amen to that, brother Joe.

For me, whenever I approach an audience or a camera I keep Joe's quote in mind.

I believe that it pays to be simple.

And that simple pays.

Tony's "Three Strong Statements" Rule

Through the years I've watched fitness videos and infomercials of every kind on TV. Some are good, some not so good.

The hosts on the not-so-good shows, in my opinion, make the same mistake every time. Besides not packing enough enthusiasm and fun into their presentations, they tell audiences that their product—an exercise machine, a stretching device—improves life in a dozen different ways, or 20 different ways. By the time they finish explaining how these 20 ways help, I can barely remember anything I've heard in this blur of claims, benefits, and promises.

People, you definitely do *not* want your product to be perceived as a blur. You want your product to stand out as clear as a diamond. No confusion, nothing to puzzle over. And most of all, you don't want to give your audience too many things to think about all at once.

To follow this advice, I use what I call the Three Strong Statements rule.

It works like this.

Instead of reciting a full-page inventory of the advantages my pillow or my sandals or my Ab Isolator delivers, in the beginning I focus on *the three most important benefits*.

Just three benefits to start with. No more. But, oh boy! How I'll drill these three benefits.

I do this by clumping the three points together and not allowing much time to elapse between the first time I mention the benefit (and show a demo) and the second time, and the third. I stay with these three points, never wandering off message. After I've drilled them thoroughly, I then add several other benefits. Then I go back to the first three points and start another round.

Examples of three strong statements:

My Micropedic Therapy Pillow

1. It cradles your head in soft comfort.
2. It's self-fluffing.
3. It never gets hot.

My Gazelle Glider

1. It's total body calorie burning.
2. It's total body muscle training.
3. It's the lowest-impact exercise machine on the planet.

Here's my favorite phrase in the world: "Now let me get right to the point!" No wasting time. No trumpets blowing. Just straight to the target with your three selling points.

Remember, three basic benefits.

You'll see the results.

"Our life is frittered away in detail. Simplify! Simplify!"

—*Henry David Thoreau, American writer and philosopher*

Who Said Short Comes Up Short?

About a half mile from where I live there's a drugstore that has a large sign displayed in its front window. The sign reads:

GOT POISON IVY?
GET ZANFEL
IT WORKS!

This is undoubtedly one of the greatest examples of a successful selling technique I've ever seen.

What's so great about it?

Simple: It's simple. Yet it also communicates big ideas.

You know, who hasn't had poison ivy? Who hasn't scratched themselves to distraction in the middle of the night? Who wouldn't crave instant relief from this torture?

Imagine that you're suffering from it right now. Wouldn't you perk up if you saw this sign? Wouldn't you jump out of your car and tear ass into this drugstore to buy it?

Take a look at the ad. No word is longer than six letters. Half the words are two and three letters. Yet despite its brevity—or because of it—its streamlined message zaps like a bullet into your brain. The first line gives you the problem. The second gives you the call to action. The third presents the solution.

I also really dig the exclamation mark at the end of the third line. A well-placed exclamation point can say more than three college professors talking for an hour.

And here's another champion, a sign I saw tacked on telephone poles in a suburb of Tampa Bay. Right away the sign catches your eye with a photograph of a cute curly-haired little doggie, a cross between a poodle, a schnauzer, and a beagle. Beneath the picture a bold-lettered caption reads:

PLEASE HELP FIND BAGEL!
MY SON JAMIE IS UP NIGHTS CRYING FOR HIM!

Then there's a phone number and address below.

Brilliant. This sign has the major elements of great salesmanship. A command. A call to action. An urgency. And most of all, a plea to people's better nature.

P.S. The sign got so many people off their butts looking for Bagel that he was eventually found. There was an article about the search in the local paper with a picture of the little boy nuzzling a very happy-looking mutt. A few choice words in the right places can move the world.

"Simplicity is the exact medium between too little and too much."

—*Sir Joshua Reynolds, British painter*

Simple Doesn't Mean Dumb

Here's still another lesson in basic, hard-driving sales power, this one from a funky homemade ad for a bar and grill I saw posted around town:

WANT TO MEET HOT GIRLS AND GUYS?
WANT TO HAVE FUN?
COME TO THE HAPPY HOUR AT FOXIE'S AT 6:00
FRIDAY NIGHTS!

Another zinger.

Another expressive exclamation point.

No long monologue—just the facts, ma'am. Sexy. Motivating. Attention-demanding. Who doesn't want to have fun? That's how your sales presentation should be.

And here we come to an important point. You want to keep it simple. You bet.

But simplicity for its own sake is neither good nor bad. What *sells* the goods are simple words that are also powerful and convincing. You need to deliver substance as well as brevity when you're writing short.

There's an old Chinese story about a butcher who worked at the castle of a king. This butcher was famous for the way he cut meat with one stroke, and for the fact that his cleaver never got dull. When he cut up an ox, "out went a hand, down went a shoulder. He planted a foot, he pressed with a knee, and the ox fell apart with a whisper."

The king heard about the butcher's incredible skill and visited him one day.

"What's your secret?" the king demanded to know.

"It's simple, sire," the butcher replied. "There are spaces in between each joint. When my cleaver finds these spaces, it has all the room it needs to make the cut. This way my cleaver strikes at the place of least resistance and always remains sharp."

Make your words simple and natural. But also be sure they have enough wit and wisdom in them to keep your cleaver sharp.

Don't Let Them Think Too Much

I'm friends with a very successful screenwriter who once told me his secret for writing great scripts: Never make your audience *think* too much.

My friend isn't saying that you should dumb down everything you write. Not at all.

What he means is that he keeps his stories so tight that all the reasoning is predone for his audiences. They don't have to stop every two minutes and ask themselves what's going on. "By the time they think over an overly complex idea and interpret what it means," he told me, "the story has moved on, and their train of attention is broken. Suddenly the magic is gone and they're no longer inside the story in a watching trance. They kind of wake up and say, 'Hey, I'm seeing a movie.' You *never* want this. You want to keep them inside."

Joe Sugarman, the legendary copywriter and inventor of dozens of standard sales techniques (such as the use of toll-free numbers to take credit cards), almost always starts his copy with a short, extremely simple phrase that captures your attention and makes you bubble over with curiosity about what he's going to say next. Here are a few of his first-line classics:

It's easy.
Judge for yourself.
It's really a shame.
Take a look here.
Losing weight is not easy.

You're stuck.

It had to happen.

Hey, why not take a chance?

Simple. Just like the words I'm using in this chapter. Have you noticed? Like Joe, most of the words I've written in the past few pages are one or two syllables long. If you convey your selling message in 100 words, try boiling it down to 50. If you do it in 50, go for 25. Less is more.

Ever hear the phrase "Keep it simple, stupid"? And what was it Tom Hanks said in the movie, *Forrest Gump?* Something like, "Stupid is as stupid does."

Simple.

Plain Speech

A man arrived late at the House of Commons, where he met Winston Churchill, who was just leaving the proceedings. The man asked if the Home Secretary had spoken yet. "Yes," answered Churchill. "He has been speaking for half an hour." The man wanted to know what the Secretary was talking about. "I don't know," said Churchill. "He has not said yet."

Obscurity in speech as well as the written word. Avoid it. Get to the point and off the pot. Here are more techniques I use to streamline my sales prose and to present my offers in easily digestible bites.

- **Practice your elevator speech.** An elevator speech is a sales pitch that eager beavers deliver to potential customers while riding up in an elevator. For a screenwriter, the deal is that if you can't compact your story into the 30 or 40 seconds it takes to get to the top floor, it's probably too complicated to make a good film. The same principle applies to selling. You should be able to explain your idea in 30 seconds or less, and tell why it will benefit customers. If you can't, it may be time to give the old drawing board a visit.

- **Concentrate a lot into a little.** General Ulysses S. Grant was a simple man. He once remarked, "I know two songs. One of them is 'Yankee Doodle' and the other isn't." I like that. One is enough. Two is too many. Three's a crowd. Four is a bore. You know what I mean.

- **Avoid overexplaining.** Avoid telling your clients or customers more than they need to know. A little is a lot when you're trying to hold someone's attention. Become a ruthless editor. Cut away the fat. Give them the beef.

- **Separate your ideas into short, natural segments.** For 30 seconds (or an appropriately brief length of time) talk about the problem. For 30 seconds talk about the product. For 30 seconds present the product's benefits. For 30 seconds say why the price is so great. For 30 seconds explain the warranty and guarantee. Then repeat it all again.

- **Use ordinary, workaday words.** Ernest Hemingway advised young writers to use simple words, and to avoid pompous, show-offy clunkers. "Poor Faulkner," Hemingway once remarked, speaking of his rival, William Faulkner. "Does he really think big emotions come from big words? He thinks I don't know the ten-dollar words. I know them all right. But there are older and simpler and better words, and those are the ones I use."

- **When writing a sales letter or ad copy, keep your sentences to 15 words or less.** This rule, used by the best copywriters, can be applied to the spoken word as well. When you're working to get a sales concept across, try talking in sentences that run four or five seconds max. You'll get people's attention better this way. Try it.

- **Keep your sales presentations unambiguous (that's the first $10 word I've used so far in this chapter, by the way).** Avoid contradictions, uncertainty, vagueness. Leave no room for questions. Real simplicity means no loose strings left dangling. No head-scratching. You get it instantly.

- **When a striking or instructive visual gets your point across, use it.** Use it instead of—or to supplement—what you say. It's the old "a picture's worth a thousand words" thing. Who wants to hear a thousand words? Have you got the time? I don't. But, oh boy, one great picture!

Remember, folks, you don't want to make them think, or hesitate, or wonder, or get confused. You want them to act!

Like the simple name of this book: *There's always a way.*

13

How to Thrill Your Audience into Buying

"Without music to decorate it, time is just a bunch of boring production deadlines or dates by which bills must be paid."

—Frank Zappa, rock and roller

"I can't tell you, but I can play it for you."

—Epiphone Guitar Company, musical instrument manufacturer

"Those who danced were thought to be quite insane by those who could not hear the music."

—Angela Monet, painter Claude Monet's wife

"We don't like their music, and guitar music is on the way out."

—Decca Records' reason for rejecting the Beatles

How to Thrill Your Audience into Buying

Food for Your Ears

Scientists at the Montreal Neurological Institute have studied hundreds of brain scans, and have come up with an amazing discovery that I want to tell you about.

The music we enjoy most, they've found, switches on the higher thinking centers of our main brain, the central cortex. The moment the good stuff starts to play we immediately think better, feel better, and work better. As Neurological Institute psychologist Robert Zatorre describes it, music triggers the "ancient circuitry, the motivation and reward system of the human mind."

This circuitry is wired in the limbic system somewhere at the center of the brain, where it rules our most basic drives, including the need for food, sex, pleasure—and *music*.

That's right; your brain considers the urge for music as necessary as your urge to eat, to have sex, and to seek pleasure.

For human beings music is food. It's universal to all cultures. When you and I are deprived of it we wither.

She Did It with Music

I had just parked my car at a lot and was walking toward the main shopping area on Melrose Avenue in West Hollywood when I heard music drifting in my direction.

I turned the corner, looked up the street, and saw something I'll never forget.

A young college-age girl was seated at a card table along the edge of the busy sidewalk. On the table in front of her was a 1950s-style Remington manual typewriter. She was plunking away at it, occasionally gazing up at the horizon as if searching for inspiration. A big sign on her table read, "The Poem Shop."

For $10 this enterprising young lady would write a page of verse on any subject you wanted. She'd do it quickly and on the spot. Songs with lyrics added were also available. These cost $20.

Now here's the interesting part. Under her table an iPod had been programmed to broadcast arias from famous operas, the perfect music to accompany her art. Before I saw her on the sidewalk, it was the music that pulled me in her direction. Other people on the block apparently had the same experience, too. Seven or eight of them were standing around her table watching her at work, stepping up now and then with their $10 bills.

"Music," says rock singer Marilyn Manson, "is the strongest form of magic."

Along with sex, it is also is one of the world's greatest financial activators. It makes people positive, happy, and hopeful—all states of mind to put them in a buying mood. "Popular music," John Lennon once remarked, "is the world's cash register."

Lyrics Count, Too

When I was performing on the bodybuilding circuit, the music of choice that my competitors used to accompany their routines was usually hard-pounding rock hits they'd borrowed from the top 10.

This was cool. But it was also herd thinking.

To be different, I chose the Bob Seger country and western tune "Turn the Page" as my theme song.

Already 10 years old at the time, Seger's song stirred up memory-lane nostalgia in the audience's mind, and offered a mellow contrast to heavy metal. I also did something with my musical routine that nobody in bodybuilding had *ever* done before. I matched the lyrics of the song to the movements in my routine.

For example, the theme of the Seger song basically says, "Here I am, on the road again. Playing the star again." These lines defined the message I wanted to convey to the audience and judges: I was on stage, playing the star. Look at me. For emphasis, every time Seger sang the refrain "Turn the page," I'd turn my back on the audience and flex my lats. Another line in the song said something to the effect that when you look at me you can't compete. When these words came on I'd point to the number pinned on my trunks.

From then on whenever bodybuilding fans heard this song, they associated the tune *and* the words with me. It became a kind of brand. This is the selling power of music.

There's Always a Way—with Music

Knowing how involved my son and daughter were in popular music, I once informed them that one day I'd produce my own music CDs and merchandise them across the country along with the biggest pop hits. When I told them this they laughed.

"You can't sing," my daughter taunted. "You don't play an instrument," my son chuckled.

They were right, of course. But only sort of. "You'll see," I said, and left it at that.

A few days later I called my manager, Ray Manzella, and told him I wanted to pull off a coup in the fitness industry that would change the way people across the country exercised. I wanted to take the best rock-and-roll songs of the past decades by the original artists and make them into personal trainer music CDs.

Exercisers are bored with the Muzak-like studio instrumentals, I told Ray. When people work out today, they may hear a song or two they like on their exercise CD. But the rest of the songs suck and put them to sleep. What they really want is exercise music that they know and love. Like the music they grew up with. Like oldies but goodies.

Ray loved the idea but said it would never fly. I couldn't afford to pay the millions of dollars in royalties for these songs, he insisted.

And he was right. It was an impossible idea.

But I had a plan.

I knew that Ray was friends with Rupert Perry, president of EMI and Capital Records in London. I was doing a lot of selling on QVC TV in London at the time, so I sent Mr. Perry a letter and asked if we could meet the next time I was in town. He wrote back and said sure.

A month or two later I met with Rupert Perry in his London office and explained my idea for an exercise CD using oldies but goodies. What, I asked him, was more motivational than a kick-ass personal trainer? Answer: kick-ass motivational music with original hits by original artists!

He got the concept right away and was pretty enthused. He picked up the phone, called the EMI and Capital Records offices in California, said I was coming out to LA, and told them that they should "give this man everything he wants."

To make a long story short, the West Coast guys green-lighted me on the project and gave me access to their entire library of past hits. They would take care of paying the royalties, too, they promised. I pinched myself. I had just been given access to all of EMI and Capital's greatest rock-and-roll hits *copyright free!*

Beat Me, Baby!

In the next few months I launched myself into project "Exercise CD" full steam ahead.

I listened to more than 500 oldies but goodies and chose the ones I thought worked best for exercise. Then I sequenced the songs on the CD so that the number of beats in each song became progressively faster.

For instance, for the warm-up section of the CD I picked songs with 105 to 115 beats per minute. Hits like "Get on Up" by the Esquires. At beginner's level I raised the count to 115 to 125 beats with "Pump Up the Jam" by Technotronic. At intermediate the music got hotter at 130 or 140 beats with "Takin' Care of Business" by Bachman-Turner Overdrive and "Rockin' Down the Highway" by the Doobie Brothers. Then advanced level hit 150 to 160 beats per minute with "All Fired Up" by Pat Benatar. That one really gets your heart going.

Finally, for the cool-off portion of the CD I brought the rhythm down to around 125 beats a minute with "Turn Back the Hands of Time" by Tyrone Davis and others. This graded sequence ensured that an exerciser's heart rate increased in a gradual, natural way from beginner to intermediate to advanced, and then down again. And it was motivating as hell to boot.

A Trip with the Kiddies to Wal-Mart

In the next year I produced a series of four exercise CDs under the name Fit Trax. One Fit Trax CD featured old rock-and-roll songs, another pop tunes, a third techno, and a fourth funk.

A few months after the CDs came out and were distributed to stores across the country, I made a trip to Wal-Mart with my kids. I guided them past the aisles of sneakers and cosmetics over to the CD shelves.

"Hey," I said, pretending that I just happened to stumble on something interesting. "Look at this, guys. Tony Little's Fit Trax CDs. Right here on the shelf at Wal-Mart. Next to a Limp Bizkit recording. Go figure!"

Their eyes popped out. They couldn't believe it.

There's always a way when you believe in yourself and then you go for it.

Do It with Music

Here are a few ideas to get you thinking music in your selling:

- Use music as a call to action. Have it playing at presentations. Include it on your web site, in your e-mails, during hold times on voice menus, in your advertisements, in the waiting room. Match the appropriate sound to the appropriate message.
- Many athletes use upbeat music to psych themselves up for an event. In the 2004 Athens Games, Olympic gold medalist Dame

Kelly Holmes played ballads by Alicia Keys like "Fallin'" and "Killing Me Softly" to get in the right performing mood.

I use music to rev myself up, too, before I do a TV interview or sales session. A few minutes before I meet a prospect or make a presentation, I'll get out the old iPod and listen to some pet favorites. It doesn't matter what they are, as long as they rock and roll and get me jacked up. I'm always surprised at how energized music makes me feel, and how these feelings improve my performance.

- Keep your favorite music going in the background when you're working at home or going over your records at night. Let the music pick you up or calm you down, whatever you need. Music diverts the mind from sensations of fatigue, another work benefit.

- I was once negotiating rights with a Peruvian businesswoman. I mentioned how much I loved the Peruvian national melody "Condor el Paso." Her eyes lit up and she started humming the tune. From that moment our negotiations went ahead without a hitch. The right music at the right time can make all the difference.

- Whenever you're feeling tired or down at work, take a few minutes and listen to inspirational or stimulating music. It will lift your spirits and make your day more sunny. When you're on your way to a sales call, put on some of that feel-good, do-good music. Your energy and passion level will jump up automatically, and you'll sell better as a result.

- And while we're at it, don't forget how important music is for the art of seduction and love. Remember, music is food. So "if music be the food of love, play on!"

14

Passion Sells

"Sales are contingent on the attitude of the salesman—not the attitude of the prospect."

—W. Clement Stone, businessman and author

"What turns a mediocre mission statement into one that makes you misty eyed every time you think of it is not a well-thought-out company policy, goal, or target market, but rather a *why* that makes it all worthwhile, a little piece of magic that comes to you in the middle of the night—a seed for great inspiration."

—Peter J. Patsula, business writer

"Motivation is a fire from within. If someone else tries to light that fire under you, chances are it will burn very briefly."

—Stephen R. Covey, business writer and motivator

Passion Sells

Change Your World

In the early nineteenth century a wealthy English fence maker named Sir Samuel Brown lived on his estate along the Tweed River. His great passion was growing roses.

Owning land on both sides of the river, Brown built a magnificent garden on the opposite bank from his home where the land was most fertile. But there was a problem. When he wanted to get to the other side of the river he had to travel several miles by horse and buggy to reach the nearest bridge. His garden was literally so near and yet so far.

This arrangement was fine for Brown while he was young. But as he aged it became increasingly uncomfortable to make the journey, and his gardening trips across the river became less frequent. As a result, his beautiful roses lost their health and beauty.

Distressed that the love of his life, his rose garden, was wilting, Brown sat down and pondered what to do.

As he sat there sipping a cup of tea and idly studying a spiderweb in a window frame, the structural beauty of the web's design suddenly triggered an idea.

"What if," he thought to himself, "I was to take some ropes, chain, and cable and build my own spiderweb across the river? Then I'd be able to cross the river with ease, and work in my garden whenever I liked."

Brown set to work, and in several weeks his weblike construction was finished. And so was born an invention that is still very much in use, and that we refer to today as the suspension bridge.

Now here's the interesting part. Brown was not a genius. He was not even an architect or engineer. He was an ordinary man *but* a man in the grip of a great passion. It was this passion that helped him change his life, and in the process, the world.

Fuel Your Fires!

Passion breathes life into everything you do; and everything you do in life can breathe passion.

What is passion, really? There's the passion that's sparked during sex, of course. What I'm talking about here is certainly related to this feeling. The two are kissing cousins. But basically I'm on a different track.

The passion I try to trigger when I'm motivating people to get off their butts and into life is a combination of human energy and human love. Bring the two together, mix them up in some vat, and presto! you have all the emotional gasoline you need to power your way through life, and to succeed at your wildest dreams.

Think of yourself as a wonderful piece of complex machinery—a jet plane, maybe. You can fly at 500 miles an hour if you want, or faster. But *only* if you have the right ingredient.

Fuel.

Without it you're out of gas and grounded on an airport runway for an eternity.

The fuel that makes your life fly is passion.

"Men who never get carried away should be."

—*Malcolm Forbes, publisher*

Reclaiming

When you were a kid, everything you did had a kick and zest to it, right? Even the most ordinary stuff like running a stick through a puddle of water or tossing a ball. You could play with a tin can in the middle of the street or a doll without a head. It didn't matter. Playing house? Playing tag? Everything was a blast! Remember how vivid these games were?

Why did they seem so real and exciting? For one reason: Because you played with *all of yourself, in the moment.* Which means you played with passion—a passion that so many of us now remember as the key to a golden past.

Then a funny thing happened on your way to happiness.

You grew up.

Now, suddenly, you were being told to mind your manners, get good grades, keep your voice down, and make sure your exuberant feelings stayed buttoned up inside. Spontaneity, animation, enthusiasm, zeal—all became no-no's. Control and seriousness were the new rules of the game. We were, after all, grownups.

Remember the old 1950s song, *Penny Candy*? It's about a rich, jaded femme fatale who's remembering back to her childhood and thinking how excited she once got over a simple piece of colored candy in a jar. And how today she has the world at her fingertips but nothing left to *love*.

"Life has been kind to me," she sings. "I've riches enough to buy whatever catches my eye. But nothing catches my eye. When I was a little girl poor and plain, all I thought about in life was in this refrain. Penny candy, candy for a penny."

That's what happens to us as we grow up and take our place in society. We lose our passion for the penny candy of life.

And we are all the poorer for it.

"Passion is energy. Feel the power that comes from focusing on what excites you."

—*Oprah Winfrey, talk show host*

Fire!

Picture this.

I come walking onto the TV screen acting *very* dignified and proper, a marvel of restraint. I don't leap onto my Gazelle. I don't fall on the floor with a pretend heart attack or drop a bowling ball on the competitor's pillow. I carefully mount the exercise machine with apologies for being late, and I begin to scissor silently back and forth on the machine with an earnest look of determination on my face. Then, purposefully, I start to count cadence the way they once taught me in gym class: "And a one, and a two, and a three. . . ."

People, just how much product do you think I'd sell if I went on the tube with this energyless, dead-dog display of self-control?

> "Passion is the genesis of genius."
>
> —*Anthony Robbins, motivational speaker and author*

Not a whole lot, baby.

Why? Because it's my passion that revs me up onscreen and releases the energy that energizes others.

Listen, I *love* what I'm selling. I absolutely *love it*! And I'm going to be in your face about it and tell you about it, Mr. and Ms. America, because I have a passion to help you and to make you strong and healthy. When I commit to a product or an idea, I completely surrender to it. I do whatever needs to be done to guarantee its success. I have no doubts once I seize a possibility. No hesitation. No negative what-ifs. Every product I choose to sell is a crusade—a campaign I'm bonded to until it meets a successful conclusion. My body is jumping around on the stage, yeah. But the real reason I have you so excited is because of the passion I have for the product, and because of the energy that's firing through my veins.

> "You taught me to be nice, so nice that now I have no sense of right or wrong, no outrage, no passion."
>
> —*Garrison Keillor, commentator on American mores*

Passion Sells

That's right, my man, my woman; passion seduces. Passion sells. Isn't it time to put it to use? To incorporate it into your own life and work when you're selling product—and when you're selling yourself?

Sure, others may not know what to make of it at first. Most of us are unaccustomed to genuine displays of honest feeling and inner fire. But they'll soon get what you're doing, and they'll respond.

Know why?

"We may affirm absolutely that nothing great in the world has been accomplished without passion."

—*Georg Wilhelm Friedrich Hegel, German philosopher*

Because your passion arouses *their* passion. You make them feel the way they *want* to feel. Your passion triggers their passion, and theirs triggers the same in others. Pretty soon things get good again for all of us. Love. Spontaneity. Happy. Excited. Alive.

Passion.

Do iiiiiiiiiiiitttttt!

Tony's Takeaways

- Passion can never be anything but sincere. If it is not sincere it is not passionate.
- Try to remember back to the time when you were a child. Remember that love of life that animated everything you did all day long? That's the passion I want you to bring to everything you do today.
- Not all enthusiasm is truly passionate, but all true passion is enthusiastic.
- Look around. Who are the people who inspire you? Who excites you? Who attracts you? What is it about them that draws you in their direction? Answer: the quality of their energy.
- Don't mistake desire for passion. Desire simply wants, but passion always loves.

15

The Neglected Key to High-Performance Selling

"Living a healthy lifestyle will only deprive you of poor health, lethargy, and fat."

—*Jill Johnson, dancer and dance critic*

"If I don't work out at least three times a week I really go off my game. I can so see the results. If I go to the gym before I go to work my thinking process is more on target, and I feel a low level high that lasts through most of the day. I feel sorry for the women in my office who announce what couch potatoes they are, and how proud they are of it. If they only knew how much not keeping themselves in good shape was throwing them off their work game."

—*Jennifer Radzski, women's fitness blogger*

"Fitness—if it came in a bottle, everybody would have a great body."

—*Cher, singer and actress*

"I never regret it when I work out but I always regret it when I don't."

—*Samson Riggs, Internet blogger*

The Neglected Key to High-Performance Selling

What You Absolutely *Must* Do to Develop the Selling Edge

A few months ago I was giving a sales presentation on TV.

In the middle of the show I got a call-in from a woman who had purchased my Gazelle Glider. What, this woman asked me with a tone of mild annoyance, was I doing working as a personal trainer *and* a salesman on TV? What does one field have to do with the other?

It was a strange question. For a moment I felt like blowing her off. I never do that to customers, though, so I answered her question in a sentence: "I sell fitness," I said, "and my fitness sells."

But this woman's question bothered me. I thought about it a lot.

In today's health-conscious United States, I asked myself, how can people be so out of date? How can they not understand that the key to good business performance is good health?

"I am sure that nothing has such a decisive influence upon a man's course as his personal appearance, and not so much his appearance as his belief in its attractiveness or unattractiveness."

—*Count Leo Tolstoy, Russian writer*

The more I thought about her question, the more I began to realize a sad fact: Nobody had ever told this woman or millions like her that our main operating tool—our own bodies— must work at peak performance with all cylinders firing if we are going to dominate in today's wildly competitive business world.

So if the woman who asked me that question just happens to be reading this book, I want you to know that this chapter is for you, and for everybody else who wants to win at the game of salesmanship and at the game of life.

Tony's Nine Reasons Why Working Out Makes Things Work Out

If you, like that lady, believe that working out is for fitness folks only, I want you to take a look at the list I've compiled. Read it, and I guarantee you'll be so motivated you'll run down to your neighborhood gym in the next 15 minutes.

Maybe sooner.

One: Working Out Makes You Look Sexy to the People You're Trying to Impress   Let's face it, first impressions are lasting impressions. If you walk into a meeting or a job interview looking burned out and off your game, you've got two strikes against you before you say "Hello."

How then do you dazzle them with healthy good looks? How do you make your skin look moist and young, and get that pink-cheeked pep? How do you keep your hair and nails in great shape, and increase your agility and grace?

How do you put sparkle in your eyes and bounce in your step?

How do you exude a sense of energy and well-being?

There's only one method I know for all the above: regular daily exercise. This is a fact, Jack! This is a fact, Jill!

Two: Working Out Keeps Your Weight under Control   Hot off the presses: A 2009 study at the University of California at Los Angeles based on an analysis of 94 brain scans indicates that obese people have *8 percent* less brain tissue than people of normal weight. And more: The brains of obese persons are biologically *18 years older* than the brains of thin persons.

"That's a big loss of tissue," says Paul Thompson, professor of neurology at UCLA and author of the study. "It depletes your cognitive reserves, putting you at much greater risk of Alzheimer's and other diseases that attack the brain."

Being overweight increases your chances of heart attack, high blood pressure, diabetes, and several types of cancers. People, there are only two ways I know to keep your tummy tamed: proper diet *and* regular exercise.

Three: *Working Out Makes You Happier at Work*   Thousands of scientific studies have proven that even 10 or 15 minutes of intense exercise a day stimulates your brain to release a bath of powerful neurotransmitters like dopamine, serotonin, and norepinephrine.

These brain chemicals fight depression, relax muscles, and stabilize mood. Along with endorphins, the body's natural painkillers, they produce that special feeling of calm and well-being you get after a workout—that exerciser's euphoria and runner's high. I can say with all honesty that I *always* feel happier and more relaxed after I spend an hour in the gym. You probably feel the same.

And isn't this what selling is all about? A relaxed, can-do, optimistic attitude? "The very definition of a salesman," says Zig Ziglar, "is a person who is both happy to see you, and happy in his own skin. You sense it in him, and it favors you in his direction."

Four: *Exercise Gives You the Energy*   Where does our energy come from? Some people think we get it from stimulants like coffee, sugar, or pills. But this is a fallacy. Stimulants simply slurp up the energy that's already inside us, which is why when you come down from stimulants you feel so tired and depleted.

True physical energy is derived from the food you eat *and* from regular physical activity.

Studies show that exercise speeds up metabolism, increases blood flow, and brings energizing stores of oxygen to the brain. It also fires up tiny centers known as mitochondria inside each cell in our bodies. These cells within cells act like miniature power plants, generating energy that sparks the nervous system and helps overcome stress and fatigue. The more you exercise, the more mitochondria your body produces. It's a seriously amazing self-generating cycle. Energy makes energy, which makes more energy. The more you work out, the better you think, feel, and do.

Five: Working Out Fights Stress on the Job   When you're stuck in traffic driving to the office, when work piles up on your desk, when coworkers are in our face, your body tenses up and bad things happen. It starts with the adrenal glands. When the pressure's on, they pump too much adrenaline into your bloodstream. This increases heart rate, raises blood pressure, and gives you those chalk-on-a-blackboard feelings of anxiety. The stress hormone cortisol is also released when stress comes, making you jumpy, irritable, and, over the long haul, downright sick. That's no good.

Exercise to the rescue. Regular workouts reduce cortisol levels, rid the blood of tension-causing lactic acid, lower blood pressure, and act as an overall counter to the nasty things that stress does to you. One more good reason to stay in shape.

Six: Working Out Prevents Illness and Sick Days   A 2005 study found that each year obesity and lack of physical activity cost American employers $11 billion in lost work hours. Each year $10 billion is spent on medical care for sick employees alone.

Many American companies have been proactive in promoting wellness in their offices or factories. Weight loss and stop-smoking plans, on-site exercise facilities, yoga classes, walking programs, healthy food choices in the cafeteria, and innovative on-site fitness devices like treadmill desks all lead to a healthier workforce.

Yet as economic times darken, higher costs have made this perk into an endangered species. And that's a shame. Businesses need these programs to keep employees happy and on the job. It would be a terrific idea if American companies avoided the penny wise and pound foolish route, and realized that spending a few dollars on company health generates big financial long-term rewards in the form of fewer workdays lost and more productive employees who simply do their jobs better.

Seven: Working Out Improves Your Sleep   Exercise calms your busy mind, and makes your body ready for sleep. It lessens anxiety and depression, two major causes of insomnia. Daily physical exertion increases the amount of time you spend in the deepest sleep states. That's a big benefit. We like that. If you're well rested, you won't nod off at your desk or head to Starbucks for sugar and caffeine. If you're well slept, you're less likely to be hungry, a plus for keeping slim. Deep sleep boosts your immune system and heightens your stamina. Sick days become a thing of the past, and you don't live in terror of the latest flu of the month. Work out to sleep well. The two go together.

Eight: Working Out Makes You Smarter   One of the most exciting discoveries made by science in the past decade is that regular exercise actually *creates new brain cells.* Known scientifically as neurogenesis, this process occurs mainly in the learning and memory centers of the brain. The more you exercise, the stronger both functions become. Working out brings fresh blood to the brain, increases circulation, and gets rid of the toxic wastes that build up from the day's mental activity. You learn better and you remember better. "Physical fitness," President John F. Kennedy once remarked, "is not only one of the most important keys to a healthy body; it is the basis of dynamic and creative intellectual activity."

Fitness, in short, makes you smarter. It helps you think better, helps you recall facts more rapidly, and helps you concentrate for longer periods of time. What incredible benefits! Take advantage of them.

Nine: Working Out Improves Confidence and Self-Esteem   There's something about a person who's in great shape and knows it. A kind of power radiates from these people. Others sense it and are attracted to it.

When you look your best; when your body image wins approving glances; when you're blasting out energy and enthusiasm; when everything feels strong, light, agile, and tawny inside—you automatically feel a whole lot better about yourself. How can you afford not to take advantage of this remarkable gift from nature? How can you afford—and I mean this in dollars and cents as well as improved health—not to keep fit?

"A man's health can be judged by which he takes two at a time—pills or stairs."

—*Joan Welsh, health writer*

Tony's Exercises for Staying Fit at Your Desk

I try to work out for an hour or so every day. But there are days at my office when I'm chained to a desk and don't have time to get to my gym. When this happens, I do the next best thing. I step myself through a series of quick, easy, at-the-desk exercises to keep limber, stretched out, and clear-minded, and to ward off the heebie-jeebies that come from sitting on my tushy too long.

Here's my 15-step routine:

1. Sitting at my desk, I extend my arms straight out in front of me. I rotate my right hand clockwise five times and counterclockwise five times. I do the same with the left hand. I then leave my arms extended in front of my body for several minutes, until they get too heavy to hold. It hurts while you're doing it, but it feels great after.

2. With my arms still extended in front of me, I turn my hands straight up so that my fingers point to the sky. I push the back of my hands toward my body, getting a good stretch on the wrists. I push for several seconds, relax, push for several more seconds, and relax. I repeat this motion 10 times.

3. I extend both arms straight out to the sides parallel to the floor. I circle both arms in one direction for 30 seconds and then the other direction for 30 seconds.

4. Standing or sitting, I clasp my hands behind my back and rotate my head as far as it will comfortably go to the left. I hold it here

for about 15 seconds, release, and turn my head to the right, holding for another 15 seconds. I do this stretch five times to each side.

5. Standing or sitting, I roll my shoulders forward five times, then back five times. Then I lift my right shoulder and push my left shoulder down. I alternate shoulders, up, down, for 10 repetitions.

6. Sitting (and with plenty of room in front of me), I extend my right foot straight out and rotate each foot clockwise and counterclockwise 10 times.

7. I stand up from my desk chair and then sit down. I repeat this motion 10 times in a row. Sounds easy. But try it.

8. Sitting, I tighten my buttocks and thighs for 10 or 15 seconds, then release and repeat several more times. For men this exercise is terrific for prostate health. For women, it's an effective butt and thigh tightener. And it actually feels really good!

9. Standing or sitting, I lean my torso as far as it will comfortably go to the right. I hold there for 15 to 20 seconds and return to an upright posture. Then I lean to the left. I repeat this exercise five times to each side.

10. Standing, I extend my arms straight up as if trying to touch the ceiling, and go up on tiptoes. I hold this posture as long as I comfortably can, then down. I repeat five times, and sometimes more if I'm bored.

11. Standing or sitting, I clasp my hands behind my back. I lean over as far as I can and hold this position with a comfortable but firm tension for around 30 seconds. I return to the normal standing or sitting position. I repeat this exercise five times.

12. Standing or sitting, I take a deep breath. I hold it in for four or five seconds, then exhale vigorously to cleanse my lungs. I inhale and exhale this way 10 times in a row. This exercise clears my head and calms me down.

13. Standing, I bend back as far as I can comfortably go, hold for a count of three, and resume my normal standing posture. I repeat 10 times.

14. Standing, I twist my torso as far as it will comfortably go to the right. I hold this position for several beats, then return and twist to the opposite side. I repeat four or five times in a row.
15. Standing or sitting, I extend both arms straight over my head and stretch toward the ceiling. I hold this position for five seconds, then relax. I repeat five times.

So that's the deal. Exercise for health, exercise for happiness, exercise for better mobility, exercise to look great, exercise to build energy, exercise to think smarter, exercise to boost your professional stock, and exercise because it's so darn much fun and because it feels so great.

And let's not forget exercise as a means for improving your love-making IQ. Then everybody—and every body—feels great!

Stay fit. It's one more way to success in life and in business.

"The first wealth is health."

—*Ralph Waldo Emerson, American writer and philosopher*

Tony's 12 Tips for Building Energy

1. Eat well. Eat lots of vegetables, go easy on the fats, and have fruit in the morning and at lunch. No sugar: sugar substitutes only. Fresh produce locally grown. Free-range, hormone-free meats. Buy your meat at a butcher shop rather than the supermarket if possible. Also, eat four to five small meals a day. It's better for weight loss and for energy building.
2. Exercise.
3. Walk whenever possible. Take the stairs, not the elevator. Walk the five blocks, don't drive.
4. Get enough sleep. Seven to eight hours a night is about right.

(continued)

5. Breathe deeply during the day, especially when you're tired, bored, or nervous. It will relax you and give you energy.

6. Spend 15 minutes relaxing every day. Sit still when you're not active. Don't waste your strength doing needless things.

7. Drink lots of water. One of the primary causes of fatigue, especially among seniors, is dehydration.

8. Take vitamins and supplements. Ask your health care provider to prescribe the ones your body and temperament need most.

9. Don't eat after nine o'clock at night. "If you sleep on a full stomach," goes a Chinese saying, "you wake up with a stone in your head."

10. Maintain good relations with everyone you live and work with. Disagreements, arguments, disputes—they are all thieves that rob your energy.

11. Don't worry. Worry is the biggest energy eater of them all. When you worry you die early.

12. Conserve your energy whenever you can. Sometimes doing nothing builds energy as effectively as doing something.

16

Tony's Top Selling Secrets 101

"The fact is, everyone is in sales. Whatever area you work in, you do have clients and you do need to sell."

—*Jay Abraham, business growth specialist*

"Reach for the stars, even if you have to stand on a cactus."

—*Susan Longacre, musician*

"If you aren't fired with enthusiasm, you'll be fired with enthusiasm."

—*Vince Lombardi, football coach*

"If you ask me anything I don't know, I'm not going to answer."

—*Yogi Berra, Yankee baseball player*

Tony's Top-Selling Secrets 101

That Famous Extra Mile

Selling isn't all that hard. You just gotta know—and I mean *know*—certain techniques that excite interest and desire, and that help you close the deal.

Some of these techniques you're probably familiar with. It never hurts to hear them again.

And anyway, it has always been my style to take standard selling games and repackage them with a "Little" spin (sorry). An old client of mine refers to this habit of mine as "the Tony It Factor."

In the end, like I said, a handful of effective techniques used in innovative ways is going to get you high marks with your customers.

We've gone over a lot of these techniques already. We'll go over a bunch more in the next few chapters. Some are easy to use, but a few take practice. As usual, it's the latter that work best. As Dr. Robert Anthony once remarked, "It's always lonely on the extra mile."

To which I'll add that it's the extra mile that always makes the difference on your way to the top.

The Secret of Asking the Right Questions

When he was at the top of his game as host for the *Tonight Show*, Johnny Carson was asked so many predictable questions by the press that he finally wrote up a list of 10 pat answers and gave them to journalists before an interview. These answers included:

1. Yes, I did.
2. Not a bit of truth in that rumor.
3. Only twice in my life, both times on Saturday.
4. I can do either, but I prefer the first.
5. No. Kumquats.
6. I can't answer that question.
7. Toads and tarantulas.
8. Turkestan, Denmark, Chile, and the Komandorskie Islands.
9. As often as possible, but I'm not very good at it yet. I need more practice.
10. It happened to some old friends of mine, and it's a story I'll never forget.

Funny, huh? But it reveals a sorry truth. Poor questions are worse than no questions.

Here, for instance, is an especially dumb question I hear salespersons ask all the time: "Sir, Madame, would you like to make a lot of money?"

Duhhhh!

Here's another one, this from an insurance salesperson: "Do you know that Benjamin Franklin once said, 'Never leave for tomorrow what you can do today'?" Zzzzzzzzz!

And another, from an investment broker over the phone: "Do you want to protect your hard-earned savings and ensure that your family is protected?"

What do you think?

A lot of salespersons are trained to barrage customers with a list of written questions designed to force positive responses. Problem is, a lot of these questions have a false ring to them. They sound canned and prepackaged, like they've been rehearsed in front of a mirror 10 minutes earlier. When you hear these spiels it's obvious that the salesperson is not really interested in finding out your true concerns, but is simply trying to maneuver you into a buying position.

"Recently, I was asked if I was going to fire an employee who made a mistake that cost the company $600,000. 'No,' I replied, 'I just spent $600,000 training him. Why would I want somebody to hire his experience?'"

—*Thomas J. Watson, founder of IBM*

Yeah. I know, the idea is to force customers to start saying the magic word "yes," and to allow the salesperson to get that all-important foot in the door. But questions like these just don't consider things from *the customer's point of view.*

Folks, you gotta ask real questions. Not questions that come out of a Cracker Jacks box. You gotta ask questions to find out what customers are really thinking, not what you *want* them to think, or *think* they should think.

A Question Should Also Be a Solution

Say you're selling a home security system.

You can ask people if they want to protect their home and children if you like, and of course nobody is going to answer "no." A question like this may scare customers, but it doesn't bring them one iota closer to buying your product. Because it only offers a problem, not a solution.

Questions that do bring them closer are questions that feature attractive benefits built into the question's syntax. Here are some examples. These questions *tell* you as well as ask you:

- Would you like a home security system that's wired directly into our 24-hour home security system?
- That gives you all-wireless operation?
- That provides a talking control panel, and away-arming facilities for when you're not at home?
- That features backup cellular transmission if your regular home phone lines go down?
- That has a guaranteed 10-minute response?
- That's rated triple A with the Home Owners Protective Institute?

I mean, come on, people, these are questions that hit on people's real security worries and needs, and then tell them what to do about it. These are the kinds of questions that sell the popcorn.

"Questions," writes Zig Ziglar, "demonstrate that the purpose of our call is to find the prospect's needs and interest while gathering information so that *together* we learn how our goods or services meet the prospect's needs (solve the problem). We communicate this message: 'Let's work together to discover the need (problem) before we offer a solution.'"

Avoid canned selling scripts. Ask questions that are spontaneous, truthful, and sincere, that include the benefits in the question itself, and that consider a prospect's genuine needs and point of view. Then fill these needs.

"We are all salesmen every day of our lives. We are selling our ideas, our plans, our enthusiasms to those with whom we come in contact."

—*Charles M. Schwab, steel magnate and founder of Charles Schwab brokerage house*

Drill More Oil Wells

"I'm not a good shot," Teddy Roosevelt once remarked. "But I shoot a lot." You get his point. The more targets you shoot at, the more targets you hit.

Here's a pop quiz for football fans.

Question one: Which pro quarterback at one time held the lifetime record for most completed forward passes?

Question two: Which pro quarterback at one time held the lifetime record for most incompleted forward passes?

Answer to both questions: Terry Bradshaw.

Terry Bradshaw liked to throw lots and lots of passes. Many of his attempts failed and many succeeded. The ones that succeeded made him immortal.

What it comes down to, really, in drilling oil wells—looking for more prospects—is a pure numbers game. More, more, and more.

The more people you meet; the more friendly and obliging you are to others; the more phone calls you make; the more letters, faxes, and e-mails you send out; the more carefully you solicit customers and keep records; the more products you offer; the more service you provide; the more frequently you're on a social network; the more you build your database of clients, suppliers, and customers; the more you keep tabs on every potential client or ally; the more business occasions you attend; the more systematic you are about covering all possible bases—the more likely you are, statistically speaking, to hit an oil geyser.

Love What You Sell and Sell What You Love

People always say I can sell anything.

This is simply not true.

I can only sell things I believe in, and that I love. When I really love the thing I'm selling, this love makes the selling easy. My enthusiasm for a product gives it a kind of magical attraction and helps the product sell itself.

In contrast, if I don't have a genuine admiration for my merchandise, people intuitively pick up on this fact. They feel it in their bones. "Hey, if *you* don't like it," they think, "why should I?" No sale.

People want to feel your energy and your passion when you're selling. It turns them on. With the best salespersons it's almost an erotic thing. If you really love your product and explain what's so lovable about it, customers will fall in love with it, too. And with you. Selling in the long run is always about selling yourself.

You can do it.

Use Repetition in the Right Way

I've talked a lot about repetition in this book, because it's cool and it works. It is, nevertheless, important to keep in mind that there's a right way to use this powerful tool and a wrong way.

The key is this. Repeat the benefits you're selling as often as you like. But use *a new and different way to repeat them* each time.

Here, for example, is an excerpt from one of my selling sessions on TV. I'll use it here to show you (1) how to use repetition in the most effective way, (2) how to successfully incorporate questions into your sales script, and (3) how to use many of the other super sales techniques I've talked about so far in this book, *all at the same time*. With a little creativity you can adapt these techniques to practically any presentation you give.

Setting: Gymlike studio
Salesman: Tony Little
Product: Tony Little's Micropedic Therapy Sleep Pillow
Script: As follows:
You ask me, people, a pillow? Why am I selling a *pillow*? And you thought I was an exercise guru!

Note the use of a question right out of the starting block.

That's right, I'm your health guru! I want you to feel good all the time. So why am I offering you a pillow, you ask?

I repeat the same question, but in a different way. I also put a question in the mouths of viewers by adding "you ask?"

Don't we all sleep? Don't we all want to feel *rested* in the morning?

More questions. I'm rousing curiosity, appealing to the listener's health needs, and churning up enthusiasm.

You know, folks, you *don't* have to spend $5,000 on one of those super adjustable beds to find out later it was only your *pillow* that kept you from a good night's sleep.

I'm telling a story. I'll repeat it later in a different way.

Okay. For example, I have long hair like lots of the ladies out there. So when it's warm and I'm sleeping, I sweat a lot. I don't *want* sweat! Do you? I don't think so! Not on your pillow! Yech! My Micropedic pillow doesn't make you sweat.

Another story, another question, and an appeal to hygiene and body image.

Plus I have neck problems.

How many of you out there have neck problems? Stiff, can't turn so well. Lots of us, right! I don't want to buy that $5,000 bed to help my neck. I tried it once, put out all that money, and it didn't help a bit. I just want a good night's sleep. So I'm looking for the perfect pillow to support my neck and head. My Micropedic pillow again.

Several more questions plus a continuation—and repetition—of the $5,000 bed story.

My pillow makes it so that, one, I don't sweat. Two, it cradles my neck. Three, it's comfortable. That's my pillow.

Note that I start out with my Three Basic Features rule: no sweat, easy on the neck, comfortable.

What about a memory foam pillow? Is this the answer? Everyone told me it was. So I went out and tried it and it's *not* the answer. Why? Because it's a dense material; it's not a soft material. It's hard. I stick my neck on it and I'm stuck. Ouchhhh! Ahhhhhh! (I jump around with my head crooked at a crazy angle.) I can't get out, I can't get out, I can't get out!! At the same time it's too hot! Really hot, this foam pillow! I'm burning up!

I'm asking questions a thousand miles an hour and answering them immediately. This technique puts a Q&A dialogue directly into the listeners' heads, raising the questions they have about the product and answering them right away. It's a very persuasive technique. I'm also clowning around with my body for a memorable visual. Physical exaggerations during demonstrations can leave a deep impression. In an indirect way I'm also repeating the same old message: You need my new pillow to get a good night's sleep.

So memory foam wasn't really the answer for me.

What about down pillows? Very expensive. Most are made with duck feathers, goose feathers. Hey, they use these feathers in ski jackets, don't they? Because they're hot. Keep the heat in. And I don't *want* my head on the pillow to be hot! I want a cool pillow! Like mine. What if I'm allergic? Goose feathers? Duck feathers? I'll blow the roof off sneezing all night.

And what happens to feathers over time? They flatten out. Who wants some flat, soggy, ugly pillow on their bed? If down flattens out, how can it support my head and neck?

A juggernaut of reasons why not to buy the competitor's product, using lots of questions. I'm also second-guessing queries in the listeners' minds. What specific details will they want to know about when they purchase a new pillow? Comfort. Appearance. Hygiene. Allergies. Therapeutic support for the neck. Most people already have these questions half-formed in their heads. I'm anticipating them and answering them before they're asked. Great system.

So I spent all the money I had on pillows that didn't do *anything* to improve my sleep or to make me cool and comfortable. Right? What'd I get? Nada!

So take a look at *my pillow*. Micropedic therapy, right? Designed with a "quad chamber design."

What does quad chamber do? Anywhere you move on the pillow, the pillow moves with you to cradle your neck. It has air flow. It never gets hot, because there are 90 million air-infused cushions in each pillow. Each little cushion is air-infused. Each cushion moves in its own area. So air is allowed to flow through it easily. It's like a mini-air-conditioning system in your pillow!

Questions, benefits, repetition.

So what do you get from my pillow versus the others out there? My pillow never gets hot. My pillow cradles you in soft comfort. My pillow never feels hard. My pillow never makes you sneeze or wheeze. My pillow is one you'll never have to fluff up, because it's self-fluffing. No matter where you move, it moves with you to support you. And it's great to look at on your bed.

Repeating the benefits in different words, and introducing a few new ones (self-fluffing, great to look at). Another question, too.

Make It New

Go on, folks, admit it! The pillow sounds really great, right? Maybe you're even thinking of buying one right now from my web site.

You see, that's the kind of selling wallop you can deliver with clear, simple explanations, believable story lines, visual demonstrations, skillful question asking, outstanding benefits, constant appeals to a listener's real needs, enthusiasm, humor, and the right kind of repetition.

So keep saying what you want to say, but in a different way each time. If you're excited about your product, they will be, too.

Pay Attention

The last word of advice for this chapter is based on a bittersweet childhood memory that I'd like to share with you. This experience taught me a life lesson that I try to keep in mind whenever I'm doing business today: Don't take anything for granted, read the fine print, and most of all, *pay attention.*

When I was 13 years old I was a member of a local 4H Future Farmers of America. Since we lived in a farm town, my mother simply assumed that one day I'd grow up to be a farmer. Go figure.

At any rate, as members of the 4H Club we visited farms, attended classes in agriculture, watched milking and hay-baling demonstrations, and learned about feeding and raising animals. One day our club leader told us that we were scheduled to attend the state fair that summer, and that every member was expected to raise an animal as a 4H project to show there.

After thinking it over I decided I wanted to raise a lamb. My mother pooled her pennies and bought me one from a nearby farm. I took the little thing home, and my father, who was still around at the time, suggested that I name her Birdie.

Being a loner as a kid and not having many friends, I spent hours playing with Birdie, and before long we were inseparable. We jogged, wrestled, romped. I taught her to fetch and do tricks. In fact, I treated her so much like a dog that after a while she practically *was* a dog.

Finally the day of the state fair arrived. When the lamb-judging contest began I brought Birdie into the ring for inspection. The other kids who'd raised lambs had to drag their animals into the ring or even pick them up.

Not Birdie. She followed me obediently to the center of the judging area, and when the judges started to examine her she sat there as still and tame as a dog at a Madison Square Garden dog show. The judges were really impressed, not only by Birdie's good behavior but with her muscular build, a result of our jogging and frisking so much. To my delight, Birdie was picked the winner and given first prize. I was so proud.

Then a terrible thing happened.

An auctioneer stepped into the ring, put a rope around Birdie's neck, and with microphone in hand started to auction her off. "Okay, do I hear $2.00 a pound? Do I hear $2.50 a pound?"

I looked at my mom, dumbfounded. What was going on?

Didn't I know that the whole point of raising a lamb with the 4H Club was to learn how to breed it for sale? she said. The auctioneer had been sent by a local meat house. My Birdie was being auctioned off for lamb chops, and the proceeds were going to—you guessed it—the 4H Club.

How did this happen?

The problem was that I simply hadn't paid attention in class when our 4H instructors explained quite clearly that the point of raising an animal for the fair was to learn how to fatten it up for meat. Somehow I'd blocked out this unpleasant fact. Or more likely, I'd been fooling around when it was being said and didn't listen.

Many years later I was telling this story to a great friend of mine, Karel Rolli. Karel listened attentively, then asked why I had named my pet Birdie. It was a lamb, after all, not a bird.

That got me thinking after all these years: Why *did* I name her Birdie?

Then I figured it out. My dad had suggested the name. Looking back I think he had an agenda that he wasn't telling me about. The real meaning of the name he suggested was not a birdie flying through the air. It was "Bye, Bye, Birdie." As in good-bye.

Boy, I really should have paid attention! Now I pay attention big time whenever I'm doing a deal.

Tony's Takeaways

- No matter how high up a person is, never be afraid to ask him or her a question. As my mother used to say, "A cat can look at a king."
- If it's an important issue, don't trust someone else to present it. Other people will not be as effective or persuasive as you at showcasing your own product or idea.
- Delegate, delegate, delegate. This statement may sound like a contradiction to the preceding entry, but it's not. When others can do ordinary work as well as you, delegate. When you can do important work better than others, do it yourself.
- I've learned to say "yes" first. Later on I figure out whether the price or the deal is worth it. I lock the opportunity up, *then* I decide if I'm able to do it, and if there's enough perks in it to make it worthwhile.
- If you come to a company to change it, don't dwell on areas that are already functioning smoothly. Focus your time and energy on things that are failing. If it ain't broke, don't fix it.

Napoleon Hill was one of my early gurus in the sales world. I found his book *Think and Grow Rich* insanely useful when I was trying to establish myself as a selling force. Here in a nutshell is Hill's simple and famous six-step goal-setting formula for making money. I've used it many times in my own work, and it always helps focus my aim and jog my inspiration.

1. Determine the exact amount of money you want to make.
2. Decide the exact goods or service you intend to provide in return for making this money.
3. Set an exact date for when you expect to gain this money.
4. Plot out a specific plan for making this money, and set it in motion *at once.*
5. Prepare a written statement formalizing all the above four steps: the amount of money you intend to make, when you intend to make it, what you'll offer for this money, and the plan you will use for getting it.
6. Read this written statement twice a day out loud, once when you get up in the morning, once when you go to bed at night.

17

Tony's Advanced-Standing Selling Secrets

"The most important thing in life is not to capitalize on your gains. Any fool can do that. The really important thing is to profit from your losses. That requires intelligence; and it makes the difference between a man of sense and a fool."

—*William Bolitho, American author*

"'Tis the set of the sail that decides the goal, and not the storm of life."

—*Ella Wheeler Wilcox, American writer*

"You can't control the wind. But you can control your sails."

—*Tony Robbins, motivational writer and speaker*

"There are a lot of ways to skin a cat out there when you're pushing product. (Apologies to all cat lovers; I'm a dog person myself.) I always ask my friends (and an occasional enemy) who are in sales to let me in on them. A lot of people in the framing business are generous and they share. I'm always amazed how many selling spins there are I never heard of till they tell me."

—*Rita Russian, businesswoman and blogger*

Tony's Advanced-Standing Selling Secrets

Show Up

Woody Allen's iconic line that "Ninety percent of success is showing up" is more than just a laugh.

It's a useful lesson that any business professional would be well advised to learn.

What does it mean, exactly?

It means that if you're not on the phone; if you're not on the list; if you're not at the party; if you're not knocking on doors; if you're not sending out flyers; if you're not pasted on the walls, making appointments, calling prospects, building your web site, social networking, and spreading the word—well, then you don't really exist at all in your field of business. "Visibility is nine-tenths of ability," a slogan-minded CEO I know likes to say.

Showing up?

It means running down every lead.

It means going to every interview, meeting, conference, trade show, and cattle call.

It means talking to everyone in your profession who counts and a few who don't.

It means penciling in reminders on your bulletin board to follow up on e-mails, letters, and calls, and then making sure you do it.

It means making phone call after call, even when prospects keep saying no.

Are you having trouble getting people to return your e-mails or letters? What restaurants do they like to eat at? Where do they get their hair done? Where do they buy their shoes or their flowers? Where do they play golf? Then just happen to show up when they're there.

A friend of mine with the amazing name Jesse James tried for months to track me down with a business proposition. No matter how hard he tried, he couldn't penetrate the iron wall my staff keeps around me.

Eventually, we happened to be in the men's room of a restaurant together. Coincidence? I don't think so. Anyway, as we were standing there side by side at the urinal Jesse struck up a conversation. In a few short minutes between the pee and the bathroom door he peppered me with so many great ideas that we ended up working together on several projects. That's how it works. They once asked Civil War General Nathan Bedford Forrest how he was able to win so many skirmishes against the greater Yankee army. "Get there firstest with the mostest" was Forrest's famous advice.

That's showing up.

Remember I told you about the car accident I had a few weeks before I was scheduled to shoot my Gazelle infomercial? How when the manufacturer told me my face was too damaged to do the show, I hopped on a plane and visited the CEO personally?

If I hadn't flown out personally and plunked my butt down there in front of the CEO, I'd never have gotten the chance to shoot the infomercial. The same when I attended that video convention in Las Vegas without knowing a soul or a thing about video production. The important fact was *I was there*, showing up. People saw me. They talked to me. Most of all, they remembered me. I returned home from that trip with several signed contracts in my pocket. If I hadn't mingled in that huge Las Vegas convention hall with all those heavy-duty video players, I would have gone hungry.

So show up. Be on the scene. Rock and roll. Why do so many people ignore this effective ploy? Are they too lazy? Shy? Busy? Is it too expensive? Too risky? You can make excuses till the snows come down. The fact is, if you don't show up, someone else will show up in your place. Law of the jungle, man.

In his popular book *Guerrilla Marketing* (Houghton Mifflin, 2007), Jay Conrad Levinson presents readers with a list written in 1885 by one Thomas Smith of London, England. Levinson doesn't say who Smith was, but I'm going to assume he was one savvy business head.

On this list Smith focuses on an advertisement. A single advertisement. But an advertisement that shows up and never goes away. An advertisement that you see and ignore time after time after time until it starts to work its magic on your mind. Here's how:

The first time a man looks at an ad, he doesn't see it.

The second time, he doesn't notice it.

The third time, he is conscious of its existence.

The fourth time, he finally remembers having seen it.

The fifth time, he reads the ad.

The sixth time, he turns up his nose at it.

The seventh time, he reads it through and says, "Oh, brother!"

The eighth time, he says, "Here's that confounded thing again!"

The ninth time, he wonders whether it amounts to anything.

The tenth time, he will ask his neighbor if he has tried it.

The eleventh time, he wonders how the advertiser makes it pay.

The twelfth time, he thinks it must be a good thing.

The thirteenth time, he thinks it must be worth something.

The fourteenth time, he remembers that he has wanted such a thing for a long time.

The fifteenth time, he is tantalized because he cannot afford to buy it.

The sixteenth time, he thinks he will buy it someday.

The seventeenth time, he makes a memorandum of it.

The eighteenth time, he swears at his poverty.

The nineteenth time, he counts his money carefully.

The twentieth time he sees the ad, he buys the article or instructs his wife to do so.

Always keep in plain sight and, if necessary, in their faces. If you're not there, you'll never bag the hare.

"When dealing with people remember you are not dealing with creatures of logic, but with creatures of emotion, creatures bristling with prejudice, and motivated by pride and vanity."

—*Dale Carnegie, motivational business author*

Hey, You're Onstage Anyway; Might as Well Act That Way

All salespeople should have a bit of the actor in them, and a bit of the entertainer. Maybe even a bit of the ham, like me.

Why? Because selling *is* acting.

I mean, you believe in your product, right? And you sincerely want to help your customers.

That goes without saying. At the same time, the things you say to sell your product may *sound* spontaneous. But if you're a serious salesperson, you've probably spent hours rehearsing your presentation, and maybe you've even practiced it in front of a mirror. Like an actor. Which is cool. Because you need all the body poise and voice skills you can get to clinch the deal.

When I sell on TV, the stuff I do looks unplanned, and in a way it is. But it's also the result of years of practice, and of trial and error. Belief in yourself makes acting easy. It's the same with selling.

Here's a list of acting-selling techniques I've found to be effective:

- **Facial expressions.** When you're with a customer, the central point of his or her visual focus will be your eyes and mouth. This means that your face is your primary selling tool. Use it with expressiveness and fluency.
- **Hand gestures.** These come immediately after facial expressions in order of importance. Use your hand and arm gestures to make a point, raise a question, express your feelings, or get a laugh. But be economical about it. I've been criticized for waving my arms too much when I get excited onscreen. There's probably some truth to this criticism. A gesture that's too broad can be a distraction.

- **Voice tone.** Another biggie. Maybe you've noticed the way I vary my voice tone when I'm selling, from a whisper to a shout. It takes a lot of practice to get this right—to project and convey the appropriate emotion in your voice for each point you're trying to make, like an actor. Some salespersons take courses in voice development and singing, and this makes sense. Your voice is your very own musical instrument. If you play it well, it exerts a hypnotic spell over your customers. If you play it badly like an off-key piano or a scratchy violin, you'll drive them into the hills.

- **Timing.** Let them handle your product, open the box, ask a question, view a certain slide at the exact appropriate moment, and you clinch the sale. Timing is all. There's a joke that's been going around the acting circuit for years.

  I tell you I'm going to say the following sentence: "Do you know that I am the world's greatest actor?"

  Then I ask you to say to me, "Really. What's the secret of your success?"

  Okay. So I say my first line, and you start to say yours. In the middle of your sentence I break in by shouting the word "Timing!"

  The joke gets the point across. Timing is all.

"We come this way but once. We can either tiptoe through life and hope that we get to death without being too badly bruised or we can live a full complete life achieving our goals and realizing our wildest dreams."

—*Bob Proctor, business consultant and personal development coach*

Make 'Em Laugh!

In the classic film *Singing in the Rain*, dancer-comedian Donald O'Connor performs a song-and-dance number that's still famous today. In it O'Connor does flips, spins, splits, and pratfalls. He gets hit on the head with a two-by-four. He puts on funny hats, plays the piano with his feet, makes love to a headless dummy, and walks into several walls, all the time selling it, selling it, selling it with his theme song, "Make 'Em Laugh!" It's one of the greatest comic routines ever, and what's especially revealing is the way O'Connor always stays on message, using all his gestures, expressions, movements, and energy to sell his humor. Take a look at it on YouTube if you have the time.

We all like to laugh, right? It makes us feel good. In the office, over lunch. Sometimes even while we're negotiating. It's one of the best ways I know to relieve tension and to get past customer resistance. Rely on hard facts and sensible reasons alone in your sales story, and a customer's conscious mind will find reasons to say no. It's a knee-jerk reaction in an age when every product for sale sounds great but few are.

Instead of burying them with facts, instead disarm them with a joke, a witty remark, a gentle wisecrack, a wry observation, a sight gag, even a well-timed funny face or crazy voice.

When I'm playing live on my infomercials, I intentionally create a collusion of humor between myself and the audience. During the show I'll clown around with the female presenters, occasionally hinting at something risqué. It never is, really. I know this and the audience knows it. We share a joke together. Everybody laughs and enjoys themselves. This positive energy comes through onscreen. I love having fun. Fun sells!

"The great thing about the way I joke around with my customers," says my friend Tony Reynolds, one of the most successful men's clothing salesmen in Beverly Hills, "is that the humor I use with them makes them feel funny, too. Humor is contagious and creates a very positive attitude in people. It softens them up and sets the stage for the selling to begin. Most people would rather see a comedy than a tragedy. Laughing makes us feel good."

Here are a few key things I've learned about humor and selling:

- **Make jokes at appropriate times.** If you have a knack for joke telling, go for it. Just be sure you tell it at the right moment. I always try to avoid tasteless and off-color jokes, by the way. Some people get a kick out of them, and they do make people laugh. Something about them can sometimes make you look a little cheesy, though. It's your call.

- **Be a good laugher.** Nothing is more flattering than when somebody laughs at your jokes. Right? It's a great way to bond with customers and to make them feel special. If the person's humor is dull and tasteless, however, don't feel you have to force a laugh. At best, consider doing what comedians do when they're trying out jokes to one another. If they like a gag they simply say, "That's funny, that's funny." Usually without a smile.

- **Laugh at yourself.** It's okay to make jokes at your own expense. Sometimes it can endear you to others. Tell a story about how you mixed up your best client's name or spilled coffee on the boss's Oriental rug—or his pants. It makes you look humble and human. However, don't do this too often. Too much self-deprecating humor can start to look like self-deprecation, period, and that's a major no-no in the business world. Everybody loves a good sport but nobody loves a loser.

- **Use body humor.** Sometimes just an expression, a gesture, a shrug, or a goofy face gets the laugh you're looking for from a customer. If you're a mimic, do a quick imitation or two when making a sales pitch. If you do voices, try one or two out on the crowd. I do both when I'm selling, and people love it. If you have a talent for humor, consider it an important tool in your selling toolbox and use it whenever you can.

"It is more important to do the right thing than to do things right."

—*Peter Drucker, business writer and management consultant*

Why Not Have Fun at It?

Have fun when you work and when you sell. Be unplanned, and if it's the right time, get goofy. When you're having fun, you're acting the way customers unconsciously want to feel inside: energized, joyous, alive. Pretty soon they're having fun along with you. Spontaneity, laughter, and good times sell product *a whole lot faster* than reciting pre-learned lines.

A friend of mine who today is a highly successful executive at Nike started out her career as a humble telemarketer. A good part of the reason for her success was the zany and creative way she approached customers on the phone.

You know what most telemarketers sound like. Robots, right? They read scripts at you, and respond to your objections with prewritten answers. This technique works okay. It plays the averages: maybe one out of a thousand will stay on the line and shell out the money.

My friend, however, approached the phone challenge from a very different angle. She would, for instance, cold call a customer, and the first thing out of her mouth would be something like this:

"I know, I know, I'm bothering you. It's seven o'clock at night and you're probably about to eat dinner or something. Right? It's a drag. Who wants to talk to some dork they don't even know when they could be relaxing or spending time with their family? I sure wouldn't. But listen, just give me a minute, huh, 'cause honest to God, I really do have a great new product I want to tell you about, and I'll be really quick. Thirty seconds is all. I promise. Pleeeeeeeeease!"

"Assuredly nobody will care for him who cares for nobody."

—*Thomas Jefferson, American president*

Numbers of people were disarmed by this madcap sales appeal and couldn't bring themselves to hang up. My friend's humor was irresistible. So was her honesty. It was something fresh and genuine, unlike the wind-up appeals we hear every day from phone solicitors. And I don't have to tell you, my friend sold 20 times more product than anyone else in her office.

If you're going to do it, have fun at it. Why not?

How to Get a Lot Back for a Little (No Pun Intended)

Last time I was in New York City I noticed a road sign on the West Side Highway.

FINES DOUBLED IN WORK AREA.
OBEY SPEED LIMITS.
IT'S THE LAW!

Fair enough. Harsh, but to the point.

A few months later I was visiting Montreal, and happened to notice a sign that conveyed a similar message. But in quite a different way:

THINK OF ROADWORKERS.
SLOW DOWN, PLEASE.

Which sign would you resonate with most? Which one would you be most likely to obey?

Be courteous. Be kind. Be considerate. Be fair. Be nice. Practice the old-fashioned virtues on the road, in the office, at home. Do it with colleagues and clients and subordinates and friends—everyone. Do it with the waitress at a business lunch, and with the guy who empties wastebaskets on your floor, and with your kids. Do it with your boss and your coworkers. Be nice to everyone.

Besides being the right thing to do, old-time virtues work. They create an environment where we can all agree and cooperate. It's the Golden Rule. Why can't we remember? I act toward you the way I want you to act toward me. When we both behave this way, we're in the groove. We're warm and happy. Productivity and morale automatically improve.

In his book, *How to Win Friends & Influence People*, Dale Carnegie tells us that Andrew Carnegie, the turn-of-the-century steel baron, paid his second in command, Charles Schwab, a salary of a million dollars a year. That's in pre-income-tax dollars. More than a hundred years ago.

Why did the steel mogul shell out so much money for a single employee?

One day Dale Carnegie personally asked Charles Schwab just this question. Here is Schwab's answer in his own words—words, Carnegie insists, that should be cast in bronze and hung on the walls of every home, store, and school.

> I consider my ability to arouse enthusiasm among my people the greatest asset I possess, and the way to develop the best that is in a person is by appreciation and encouragement. There is nothing else that so kills the ambitions of a person as criticism from superiors. I never criticize anyone. I believe in giving a person incentive to work. So I am anxious to praise but loath to find fault. If I like anything, *I am hearty in my approbation and lavish in my praise.*

When I'm dealing with people at work, both the highest placed and the lowest, I try to follow Schwab's model. I go out of my way to say "please." I make a point of saying a genuine "thank you" no matter how small the favor. "Thank you" is the most powerful phrase in today's society.

When I call someone on the phone, I ask whether it's a good time to talk. If not, I thank them and call back later. When I say good-bye I'm cordial no matter what negative turns our conversation may have taken. People remember good-byes, especially if they're sincere.

I try not to talk too loudly on my cell phone when others are around. If I receive a call at a business lunch or dinner, I ignore it or get up from the table to talk. I don't use my BlackBerry in meetings. It's rude.

When I'm dealing with new contacts or clients, I do my homework on them. I find out in advance where they're from, what they like to eat and drink, what restaurants they prefer, how and where they like to conduct business. Sometimes a Google search is all that's needed. In a business meeting I look for mutual interests to share. I ask sincere questions. I inquire about the client's family, sports interests, hobbies, and business life. I try to care. Because we need to care.

A genuine concern for another person's feelings is a rare thing in today's marketplace. The American cult of rudeness has largely shouldered it out of the picture. But believe me, at heart people are *hungry* to be treated with kindness and concern, and they all notice it when you do. Some even respond in kind.

We have to start somewhere, don't we? With "random acts of kindness." Here's a saying I keep tacked to my bulletin board: "Be nice to people going up. You'll meet them coming down."

Say It without Saying It

Sometime in the early 1970s a new science went pop.

With the publication of Julius Fast's book *Body Language* (M. Evans, 1970), people began to realize that their opinions of others—and others' opinions of them—were based less on words, and more on the nonverbal cues that are broadcast by a smile, a frown, crossed arms, blinking eyes, a leaning forward, a stepping back.

Up until this time people sensed this hidden language, but mostly on a visceral and unconscious level. Now it had been "discovered" by psychologists, and was out there revolutionizing the way business was done.

I was just a kid when the body language thing got popular. Being a physical type, I remember being impressed by the fact that in the real world people pass information on to one another more by the way they use their bodies than by what they say. In sales and entertainment, once you start looking for it, you see people sending unspoken signals to each other all the time. Knowing how to read these signals can make or break a relationship, a presentation, or a deal.

For instance, when Tony Robbins talks to audiences in his videos he uses a neat trick. Suddenly he'll snap his fingers. The sound and movement of this gesture jolts viewers out of their trances, and forces them to pay attention.

In the latest *Batman* movie, the late Heath Ledger playing the Joker made superb use of body language with a simple, horrifying trick. Whenever the camera was on him he'd move his tongue in bizarre and repulsive ways. He'd dart it out, run it along his lips, move it to the right and to left. It was hypnotic. You couldn't stop looking at it.

In your own career there are thousands of ways you can use your body as a selling tool to get people's attention, and to reinforce whatever message you want them to hear.

Start with steady, friendly eye contact. This, common wisdom says, is what honest people do. Dishonest people, common wisdom also says, are shifty eyed or look down when they speak. Even if this notion isn't always true, it's the way people perceive these expressions and that's what counts. When I'm doing a show, I try to look directly into the camera as much as possible. Even over TV, steady eye contact creates confidence and builds trust. One study showed that audiences rated lecturers who looked straight at them as "sincere," and speakers who looked into the distance as "insincere." Failing to make eye contact is taken to mean you're not paying attention, or worse, that you're playing head games. People notice these behaviors and react.

When appropriate, I also try to make direct physical contact with my clients whenever I can with a touch on the arm or a pat on the shoulder. If the timing is right and the moment fitting, touch can communicate positive feelings far more directly than words.

Customers respond best to salespersons who sit or stand in a relaxed, open way with nothing crossed and few signs of inner tension. Studies show that people in business meetings tend to mimic one another's states of tension and relaxation. When Jill tightens up, Jack unconsciously does the same. When Jill relaxes and takes a deep breath, Jack follows. You know how contagious yawning is? It's the same with the rhythms of tension and ease. Watch people you're dealing with and you'll see.

Smile whenever possible—but sincerely.

Some years ago research psychologist James V. McConnell at the University of Michigan studied the human smile response. McConnell found that people who smile tend to do better at work, are more effective parents, and enjoy life more. He turned up the interesting fact that physicians who look glum at the office are sued for malpractice *twice* as often as doctors who maintain a cheery appearance. McConnell cited a study revealing that 80 percent of parents of juvenile delinquents were habitual nonsmilers.

Psychologist Robert Zajonc is also known for his studies on smiling. Zajonc recently discovered that smiling actually cools the blood in a person's face, and that it releases serotonin, the neurotransmitter responsible for well-being. Old trick: Whenever I'm about to go into a meeting I smile for 20 or 30 seconds before I enter the room. This simple act instantly puts me in a positive frame of mind. When I walk into the meeting the traces of the smile are still on my face.

When talking or listening to others, avoid rapid blinking. I do it sometimes and have to catch myself. Rapid blinking can mean you're nervous or dishonest. One study showed that when President Richard Nixon told a lie at a press conference, he blinked 30 percent faster than when he was telling the truth. But don't jump to conclusions. I've noticed that when a client blinks rapidly it can also mean he or she is considering my ideas. When this happens I let them blink away and just wait.

Nod your head yes to reinforce what you're telling clients or customers. It's hard to think "no" when someone's nodding at you affirmatively. If you nod and the person nods with you, you've practically made the sale. If others lean toward you when you speak, you have their sympathetic attention. If they lean back though, they may be symbolically trying to get away from you or, more likely, from what you're saying. Be attentive to raised eyebrows, hunched-up shoulders, a wrinkled brow, averted eyes, a bored stare, or a puzzled facial expression. The sender may be saying "Convince me more," or even "No deal."

Clenched fists suggest nervousness or anger. Crossed arms classically mean the person is closed to your ideas. Crossed legs say the same. Be wary of placing your hand across your mouth when you're talking. It can be interpreted to mean you have something to hide.

Be especially careful of the steely stare. Some professionals I know in the entertainment industry use it as a power ploy. You've undoubtedly met power trippers like these yourself. But I've seen the steely look backfire and turn people off. It's said by historical eyewitnesses that one reason Hitler successfully browbeat his adversaries was because his stare was so spookily fixed and unmoving. One diplomat remarked that he never blinked. That's good for destroying the world, but not so great at the company party.

Remember, every move you make in a social or business setting sends a message to others about who you are, what you think, and what you're after. Even if people are untrained in the arts of interpreting body language, they'll instinctively read your body projections, and respond accordingly. The great football coach Vince Lombardi always told his players, "Look good getting off the bus, and then play a heck of a game!"

In other works, look like a winner physically, behave like a winner socially, and you'll always *be* a winner.

Tony's Takeaways

- Confidence, energy, enthusiasm, positivity, and a passion for selling are your building blocks for success.
- Everything that has to do with selling has to do with life as well. The way you approach a challenge in the marketplace or on the job is the way you'll approach everything else—your family life, your love life, your sports and pastimes—everything.
- There are many roads up the mountain to success at the top. There's also a road that's just right for your temperament and needs. Your job is to look for it and then start climbing.
- The basic lesson of this book has been the lesson of my lifetime as well: There's always a way. Make this phrase part of your plan for daily living. Do it now!

18

Tony's Totally Stupid, Idiotic, Useless Sales Secrets

"Remember . . . the worst thing you can do is CHASE. Selling is all about ATTRACTION. This doesn't mean you sit on your duff and watch the world go by. But what it does mean is that you don't sit by the phone waiting for that elusive customer to make your millions."

—*Kim Duke, business writer and sales trainer*

"Salesmanship is limitless. Our very living is selling. We are all sales-people."

—*James Cash Penny, founder of J.C. Penny*

"Don't sell it in gray. Sell it in color. Don't yell. Sing instead."

—*Richard Cash, public relations man*

"If you work just for money, you'll never make it, but if you love what you're doing and you always put the customer first, success will be yours."

—*Ray Kroc, founder of McDonald's*

Tony's Totally Stupid, Idiotic, Useless Sales Secrets

Made You Look, Made You Look!

Didn't I? And did I get you?

More important, do you get the point?

How could anyone not want to keep reading when they come to a chapter with the unlikely title "Tony's Totally Stupid, Idiotic, Useless Sales Secrets"? Even though it's a seemingly negative statement, it has mighty grabbing power and is loaded with the trade secrets I've been telling you about, such as:

Step out to stand out.
Take risks.
Think outside the box.
Choose short, high-impact words.
Use humor.
And so forth.

So don't pee in your pants. The motivational advice in this chapter is as good as in any other part of the book, and maybe better. Just bear in mind that you can get people to notice you in a whoooooole lot of different ways when you're trying to get your product sold. I know I'm repeating myself, but didn't I tell you? Repetition, repetition, repetition.

"Let everyone engage in the business with which he is best acquainted."

—*Propertius, Roman historian*

Study Your Customers, Study Your Competition

Once in his producing days in Hollywood the notorious Howard Hughes was making an epic movie filled with tons of costumes, sets, and history book characters. During the shooting, an assistant came up to him and questioned an historical fact in one of the scenes. The assistant suggested that they send a staff member to the library immediately to find out if the detail was accurate. Hughes bellowed at him, "Never check an interesting fact."

In sales, like I told you, I try to think a little like a military guy. It's no coincidence that Sun Tzu's 2000-year-old *The Art of War* is used by serious business individuals around the world. "If you know the enemy and know yourself," the Chinese sage wrote, "you need not fear the result of a hundred battles."

Your customers aren't your enemy, obviously. But they are the target of your advance strategy, and in this sense should be understood as well as possible. Unlike Howard Hughes, you *do* have to check your facts.

For example, I keep a steady eye on demographics. What population segments are buying my goods on TV? What's their gender? Their average age? Their income and education level? What cultural backgrounds do they represent?

What about surveys? Exploratory customer research? Market studies? They can all help.

And simple word of mouth. Guerrilla marketing. Keep your ear to the ground. Ask questions. Talk to potential buyers. Listen to their stories. What are your customers clamoring for these days? What are their gripes? What new products are flying off the shelves? What are the latest hot buttons you can push to increase sales? You'll learn a lot about your customers by tuning in to the local buzz.

Research your competition. Visit their stores. Read their literature. Study their web sites. Talk to their staffs. What are their strengths and weaknesses? What do they do better than you do? Where do you need to improve things to compete?

Study your competition, then make your commercial offering a *little* better than theirs. Improve one widget, list one extra benefit, beef up your guarantee, then tell people all about it. When I was selling my Micropedic pillow on the Home Shopping Network, I decided to add two extra benefits to my pitch. These were: (1) The pillow doesn't flatten out on the bed. (2) The pillow stops you from sweating.

The next time out on TV, sales of the Micropedic pillow increased by 10 percent. That's a lot. And all I did was make a slight improvement to an already successful sales pitch. Sometimes that's all you need to make your sales take off.

The raw marketing fact of life is that whatever goods or services customers want today, they probably won't want tomorrow. Markets for just about everything, especially luxury and discretionary items, are volatile. One size never fits all in selling.

Make Your Customer the Star

Every day from 1945 to 1957 the television curtain went up for *Queen for a Day*.

On this mother of all TV reality shows, the host, Jack Bailey, would interview four middle-aged female contestants who competed with each other for the most tragic, tear-jerking life story. Poverty, widowhood, sickness, disabled children, fire, flood, even the hint of rape were typical scenarios.

At the end of each show the audience then chose the most outstanding sob story by ringing the "applause meter." The winner was crowned and awarded a range of goodies like a night on the town, a cosmetic makeover, or more darkly, a nurse to take care of her kids while the "Queen" went to the hospital for an operation.

I only saw later redos of this show, but the idea always seemed a sound one to me from a selling perspective: Make your customer king or queen for a day.

Whenever I want to sell anything to anyone, I focus *completely* on the buyer's needs.

What do they want most? To get a great product, of course. But on a motivational level they also yearn:

- To be taken seriously.
- To be listened to.
- To be treated with respect.
- To be admired.
- To be prosperous.
- To be happy.
- To be loved.

When I take call-ins on TV or write-ins on my column and web site, I try to respond to these needs. For example, here's a write-in I recently received:

> I'm not so lucky with love, and every time I get dumped I dive into the nearest carton of ice cream or reach for one of those double-dipped Drumsticks. I really want all that sugar at the time, but it messes up my mood. I already know a lot about emotional eating, but somehow I just can't get over wanting this sugar fix.

Here's my answer. I address this woman's needs. I also talk to her heart, and try to make her feel special. Because she is:

> My three words for success in any endeavor are: conceive, believe, achieve. These can be your ticket to getting off the roller coaster of binge eating. You're a really bright woman and I know you can do it. It just takes some discipline, which I know you're capable of. You must believe you can do this. Believe with all your heart that you are the beautiful, strong-willed person that you are. With vision and belief comes achievement. You can win this battle—don't give up the fight.

If you change your customer's mindset, you change his or her life as well. Always listen to a customer's story and read between the lines. Between the lines is the place you'll find where the customer really lives, and what he or she wants and needs.

"If you put the product into the customer's hands it will speak for itself if it's something of quality."

—*Estée Lauder, founder of Estée Lauder Companies*

Criticism: File It, Use It, or Forget It

You wouldn't believe the hostile things people say to me on my web site or on call-in shows. They accuse me of being a phony. They tell me I'm a girl dressed up as a boy. They tell me I'm a big-mouthed slob, or that they want to beat me up. One guy challenged me to a knife fight.

There are some nut-job dudes out there, I gotta tell you!

But when people confront me with anger and hostility, I have my own way of responding that defuses their negativity.

For one, if callers are angry but nonetheless sound sane, I'll listen carefully to what they have to say. If it makes sense, I'll thank them. Then on to the next caller. If the criticism is useful, I may then incorporate it into my business or my living agenda. If not, remember the famous Italian saying: forgeeeeeeeet about it.

Say an angry lady phones me while I'm on a live call-in show. The first thing I do is ask her name. Right away this knowledge arms me with a valuable tool. A person's name is their most prized possession.

As a rule, you can tell in five or ten seconds if callers are going to go hyper-hostile on you. When I see it coming, before callers have time to work themselves into a super lather, I stop them cold by calling out their name. *"Mary Ann, Mary Ann—I have something really important to tell you!"*

This method works really well. Almost everybody ceases work when they hear their name called out. Once I slow them down this way and grab their attention, I then try to win their friendship.

"Mary Ann, do you know that you motivate America! You make the products I sell great! 'Cause you call in like this! You care! You want to talk about it, to know more about it! To give your opinion in this free country of ours!"

Right away I put a positive, feel-good set of ideas into Mary Ann's head. I make her the star.

Or say someone calls in angry that they aren't getting results from an exercise product. I ask if they've called our help line and spoken to their free personal trainer.

They always say no.

"No! Why not?"

"I forgot."

"Then do it right now, Mary Ann. Here's the number. Call after you hang up so our trainer can get a sense of your body type and give you the advice you need. Go on, Mary Ann, do it now! It's free for being my customer!"

Right away I feel her attitude improve. I'm using my positive energy and enthusiasm to change her mindset from negative to positive.

And, you know, when Mary Ann calls in with a complaint, this also means that deep down she's still interested in my product. She hasn't given up on it yet. Usually she just needs to know more about it, and it's my job as salesman to transform her negative question into a positive solution. At the end of these conversations we're usually friends. Mary Ann is now eager to try the item, and to tell her friends and family what a *great* product the guy on TV with the ponytail is selling.

Turn hostile criticism into constructive advice, complaints into profit, adversity into victory, negatives into a positives.

There's always a way.

Success Is in the Details

There are no clocks in Las Vegas casinos. You are far more likely to part with your money if you gamble in a timeless world. A little thing, but it brings big dividends for the gambling clubs.

Smart politicians rent halls for press conferences that are a little too small to hold all the reporters attending. This way the next day, when reporting on the conference, the press writes, "So-and-so talked before a standing-room-only audience of reporters today."

Napoleon once remarked that he beat the Germans at the battle of Austerlitz because "I knew the value of five minutes." Details.

For many years drivers complained about how difficult it was to keep coffee in the car without spilling it. Where to put the cup? Then General Motors installed cup holders in its new line of vehicles, and sales soared. The power of the small.

When DeWitt Wallace was looking for a location to build the headquarters for his new magazine, *Reader's Digest*, he chose the town of Chappaqua, New York. He then did something odd. He set up the magazine's post office box in nearby Pleasantville, and used it as the *Digest's* mailing address. Know why? Because when readers saw the very friendly name "Pleasantville" in the magazine's promotional materials, they were more inclined to subscribe. This is one of the many details that helped *Reader's Digest* become the most popular magazine in the world.

So dot your i's and cross your t's, folks. When you do little things that nobody else is doing, you do a lot.

When I'm arranging my product shots for TV, it's essential that every piece of merchandise be perfectly positioned, from the product to the instruction brochure. I make sure that the exercise machine is placed at the exact right angle to give viewers maximum visibility. I monitor what my demonstrators wear, how they fix their hair, the colors on the walls on the set. I show the object I'm selling in the round. Front and back. That's important and often neglected.

Show—don't tell, but show—the small but appealing benefits that your product offers.

Do it with demonstrations, photographs, video clips. Show the kitchen appliance mixing dough in a bowl, a pretty woman sleeping peacefully on a pillow, a photo of a house that's for sale. Use strong graphics to pound home your selling points. Show how the product helps in the kitchen, in the shop, at the desk. Tell listeners how easy it is to obtain the product.

Appeal to the senses. Let them touch your product, taste it, pinch it, pick it up. Play stimulating music during presentations. Support your claims with testimonials. Let experts speak approvingly of what you're selling. It all adds up and helps convince.

When I first started making fitness videos, I watched how others did it. One thing that really bothered me was that exercisers in these videos counted their repetitions out loud. I hated that "one, two, three, four" thing of aerobic dance exercises. The counting just irritated me. It was a little thing, but it got on my nerves. Maybe it got on viewers' nerves, too, I thought.

So I invented what I called a "time clock graph," and positioned it onscreen under each exerciser. The graph counted down the number of seconds of workout time that was left in each set for the beginner, the intermediate, and the advanced. Besides being nice to look at, the graph was motivating and helpful. See, Mr. and Ms. Viewer, you have only 15 more seconds left to go! You can do it!

It was a tiny innovation, but it was totally new and it helped sell videos. When you're selling, remember: There's no such thing as a little thing.

Have Your Sizzle and Eat It, Too

It's one of the great phrases ever coined in advertising: "Sell the sizzle, not the steak."

The thing is, though, to my mind when I offer a product, I like to sell both the steak *and* the sizzle. Know what I mean? Why be exclusionary?

The sizzle is the emotion you embed in your words and pictures, and the corresponding feelings of desire and need they evoke in customers. Remember, people don't buy the product per se. They buy what the product can do for them.

If you're selling sausages, describe the tantalizing aroma they emit when they're cooking on the grill. If you're selling umbrellas, show how they protect you from dangerous cancer-causing ultraviolet rays. If you're selling dog food, show a picture of a doggie wagging his tail and wolfing down a bowl of canned meat that looks so delicious you'd like to try it yourself.

Show people what their lives will be like when they buy your idea, your merchandise, your dream. Show them how much better existence will be when they do what you're telling them to do. The sharper you draw a positive picture of benefits, the more people will respond to your appeals.

I remember years ago driving across the great Mojave Desert. It was a 106-degree day near Needles, California, which is often the hottest city in the United States. My air-conditioning was struggling to keep up and was losing.

As I drove along mile after dehydrating mile, I happened to pass a large hand-printed signboard propped up along the side of the road. It read: "Ice Cold Lemonade ahead at Maude's Market." Beneath the words was a colorful drawing of a glass of lemonade with ice.

A few miles later I passed a similar sign. This one offered, "Ice Cold Watermelon ahead at Maude's Market" with a big red watermelon slice below. A few minutes more and there was another sign: "Home Made Ice Cream ahead at Maude's Market."

By the time I reached Maude's a few miles down the road, believe me, my thirst had become so overwhelming that I pulled over and almost sprinted into the store, buying everything cold in sight. It was more than the heat that had sizzled me.

"One of the most successful salesmen for popcorn machines," writes Maxwell Droke, an early motivational writer, "says that his first step is to 'make the merchant's mouth water for crisp, tender flakes of snow white popcorn, flavored with pure creamery butter.' He makes his prospect *hungry* for popcorn, then proceeds to convince him that there are plenty of folks who will respond to the same hidden hunger, and trade their nickels for delicious popcorn."

That's the sizzle.

Important? You bet.

"You Gotta Know the Territory!"

These are the famous lines salesman Professor Harold Hill sings in what's been called the "Broadway salesman's musical," *The Music Man.*

And you do. You gotta know the territory. You gotta know your product and you gotta know your customer. If you're going to give it sizzle, first find where the sizzle lies.

A perfect example of *not* knowing the territory took place in August 2009 when the chief executive of Whole Foods Market, John P. Mackey, made a speech in which he objected to government involvement in health care.

Mr. Mackey had a perfect right to his opinion, of course. But sometimes discretion is the better part of valor, especially in business. The upscale, liberal, crunchy granola crowd that patronizes Whole Foods was instantly up in arms over this speech. The Internet, Twitter, Facebook, listservs, blogs, and Whole Food's own electronic forum all zinged with messages from offended customers, many of whom were urging buyers to boycott Whole Foods and to shop for their organic goodies elsewhere.

A few days later Mackey publicly explained that he was voicing his own opinion, not that of his company. But by now the damage was done. Complaints flooded Whole Food's communications centers, and they were pressured to spend the next few weeks fielding angry questions and pacifying angry customers. Chief Executive Mackey clearly did not know the territory.

In contrast, a grandmaster of *knowing* the territory was a gentleman named Ray Kroc. No man ever knew his product or his customer better than Ray Kroc.

A longtime traveling salesman, this remarkable man once worked for room and board at Ray Dambaugh's Restaurant in the Midwest simply to learn everything he could about the restaurant business. During his early years he worked as a paper cup salesman, a jazz musician, and a radio announcer. Finally, he went on the road selling Multi-Mixer milkshake machines to mom-and-pop restaurants across the United States.

In his early 50s, after spending many years learning the selling trade and studying the way local eating establishments delivered food to patrons, Kroc visited a small but highly successful hamburger chain run by two brothers, Mac and Dick MacDonald.

These two self-made marketing whiz kids had developed a highly mechanized and efficient program of food preparation that they dubbed the "Speedee Service System." They were already selling franchises for their MacDonald's restaurants, though on a modest scale.

Immediately realizing the supersized potential in the automated hamburger business, Kroc went to work for the MacDonald brothers as head of franchising. While he worked he also spent time in the company kitchen, studying the patty-making machines, improving them, fixing them. After a few years he grew tired of the MacDonald brothers' reluctance to open more stores, and he bought them out. Once the business was his, he surgically removed the "a" from the "Mac," changing the chain's name to McDonald's.

Ray Kroc then went on to apply Henry Ford's assembly-line techniques to the food business, single-handedly inventing the fast-food industry in the United States, and building the largest restaurant business in the world.

Part of his genius was advertising. No one had ever seen anything like it. He blitzed the airways 24/7, making his hamburgers sound like filet mignon. Yummy patties, choice meat, mouthwatering cheddar, extra lettuce and pickles, all at cheap prices with fast, friendly service, drive-in purchases, no waiting for reservations, and kid friendly—you'd find it all at McDonald's.

It was a new and amazing way to merchandise a product. Kroc understood that the United States was a country of people in a hurry, people who liked to eat out, people who liked a bargain, and people who in the long run preferred plain old juicy American food on their table. He knew that hamburgers could be more than a lump of meat. They could be pure sizzle.

He knew the territory.

"I was 52 years old," Kroc wrote. "I had diabetes and incipient arthritis. I had lost my gall bladder and most of my thyroid gland in earlier campaigns. But I was convinced that the best was ahead of me."

Niche Marketing

In 65 B.C. Marcus Licinius Crassus was a businessman on his way up in the city of Rome.

Noting one day that Rome had no city fire department, Crassus recruited an assortment of ex-soldiers, laborers, and thugs, organized them into crews, equipped them with a fleet of portable water and hose wagons, and told them to show up wherever a fire broke out.

A good idea. Filling a need. Finding a niche. But Crassus went a little further than this.

Once arrived at the scene of the blaze, the foreman of his crew was instructed to find the owner of the burning building and make him an offer he couldn't refuse: Sell the building at 10 percent of its value or the firefighting crew would leave the premises and allow the building to burn to the ground.

Needless to say, most owners chose to salvage at least something out of the disaster, and sold. Crassus soon owned a quarter of the city, and became the richest man in Rome.

Heartless and criminal? It goes without saying. Don't do it in front of the kiddies.

But the idea behind it is a solid principle of business. Find a need and fill a niche.

In today's gloomy economic environment, there's a lot of untapped opportunity out there for profit. When one thing goes down in the business world, another goes up.

Housing prices are in the hole. If you own a house it's a bad time to sell. But if you have some ready investment capital stashed away, it's a great time to buy. Automobiles are expensive, and the recession hasn't helped dealerships drop prices that much. Bad for some, good for others. This may be the perfect time to get into the used car business.

I told you in an earlier chapter how when I decided to sell food on TV the execs at the Home Shopping Network insisted it wasn't a good idea. Viewers buy their food at supermarkets, they said. And anyway, food sales is one of the hardest categories to crack on TV.

I assured them that audiences *would* buy food on TV as long as I could convince them that my product was unique, that it was healthy in a way the other food products weren't, and that they couldn't find it anywhere else. I then went on the air and started selling bison hot dogs and bison hamburgers like crazy. Listen in:

"Here's why you need it, people. Do you have high cholesterol? This is the meat for you. Bison has 3.5 times less fat than beef. It has less fat than a chicken breast. And it's a *hamburger*.

"Afraid of getting poisoned by all the hormones and chemicals they put in supermarket meats? My bison are all uninjected and grass fed, unlike most supermarket lamb, pork, and beef.

"Afraid of getting fat? My bison burgers have four times less saturated fat than any other popular meat.

"Coronary problems? No problem. Bison is the only meat recommended by the American Heart Association. If you've got a tricky valve or pesky blood pressure and you like to eat meat, bison is your dish. It's the healthy red meat alternative."

Right down the list: unique benefit after unique benefit. This is the only meat on the market that does all these things for you. You won't find this product on any supermarket shelf. Look better and feel better. Buy it now! In one day on the Home Shopping Network I sold 173,469 hotdogs and 171,827 burgers, cashing out at over $1.4 million for a day's work. Thank God and HSN for giving me a chance.

Create a need and fill it.

There's a story about an enterprising salesman who managed to get his foot in the office of a wealthy physician.

First the salesman tried to sell the doctor his line of shoes. The doctor didn't need shoes. Then hats. The doc had plenty of hats. What about a nice suitcase? Never travel. Binoculars? What the hell for?

Finally, the doctor grew tired of the salesman's persistence and ordered him out of his office. At the door the salesman turned and smiled. "I know exactly what you need, sir," he said.

He reached into his bag and brought out a small brass plate with an inscription on it. It read:

NO PEDDLERS OR SOLICITORS ALLOWED!

The doctor laughed, admitted that this was an item he really could use, and bought the brass plate immediately.

Find the need and fill it.

What a Manager at Wal-Mart Said about His Boss—and Founder of Wal-Mart—Sam Walton

"He is a master at erasing that 'larger than life' feeling that people have for him. How many always start the conversation by wanting to know what *you* think? What's on *your* mind? . . . It's almost like having your oldest friend come just to see if you're okay. He never let us down."

—*Quoted in Great Motivation Secrets of Great Leaders by John Baldoni*

Tony's Six Tips for Dealing with Criticism

1. Listen to the criticism carefully before you respond. When criticism comes your way, apply the 80/20 rule. Listen 80 percent of the time, and talk 20 percent.

2. One type of criticism is motivated by the impulse to help, the other by the urge to feel powerful and in control. Learn to tell the difference between the two when you criticize and when you're criticized, and act accordingly.

3. See constructive criticism as feedback, not a complaint. If the criticism you receive seems accurate and appropriate, use it.

4. Don't get angry at criticism. If you do, you make the criticism into a self-fulfilling prophesy.

5. Try not to take criticism personally. If it's mean-spirited, the problem is more with the criticizer than with your own deficiency.

6. If the criticism seems reasonable, write it down. Look at it from time to time. Evaulate it. If the shoe fits, wear it.

Tony's Takeaway

- There's nothing wrong with fear, as long as you make it your ally. Myself, I'm always afraid. I'm afraid every time I go on the air. Every show scares me. I don't know why. Maybe it's because I'm so afraid of losing. But fear also makes me sharp to my game. It makes me do more things than most people would ever do because I am afraid I'm going to let people down. And this is what makes me successful. You can use fear either to cripple you or to empower you. I choose the latter.

19

Begin It Now!

"A mistake is simply another way of doing things."

—*Katharine Graham, publisher of the Washington Post*

"Find out who you are, and do it on purpose."

—*Dolly Parton, country and western singer*

"Build a dream and the dream will build you."

—*Robert H. Schuller, motivational writer*

"It was character that got us out of bed, commitment that moved us into action, and discipline that enabled us to follow through."

—*Zig Ziglar, motivational business writer*

Begin It Now!

Time to Go to Lunch

In a small town in rural New Hampshire an enormous chunk of rock has just broken off from a mountainside and rolled down onto the highway below. The boulder is enormous, some 25 feet high and 25 feet wide, and it is now perched in the middle of the main road leading in and out of the town.

To move this boulder will be an enormous task. It will take several munitions experts to blast the rock to pieces, a bevy of cranes and bulldozers to push the debris into a mound, and a fleet of trucks to haul it away. The job will take many days, and will cost the town hundreds of thousands of dollars. The town council convenes and decides to call in bids from local contractors.

The bids come pouring in, with estimates ranging from $100,000 to half a million dollars.

Then, just before the bidding closes, an estimate arrives from a contractor whom nobody knows, and who works in a town an hour away.

His price: $25,000.

Estimated time to do the entire job: half a day.

The town council is amazed at this audacious offer, and deeply suspicious. They call the contractor down to town hall and start grilling him. How, the council wants to know, does he intend to do such a huge job for so little money—a job that other, more experienced contractors insist will cost far more than his estimate, and take several weeks to complete?

The contractor smiles and says he has a plan. What it is he won't say. It's his secret. "Just give me a chance," he asks the board, speaking with impressive passion and assurance. "If I don't complete the work for the estimated amount of money in the estimated period of time, you don't have to pay me *a penny*. Just get somebody else to do the job."

The council members talk over this proposition and decide that they have nothing to lose.

They hire the contractor on the spot.

The next day at sunrise the contractor pulls up to the boulder driving a small backhoe. The townspeople and council members look on in amazement. Then they start to laugh. The contractor must be playing a practical joke on them. If he thinks he can move this gargantuan rock with this small piece of machinery he is clearly out of his mind. And if he does by some miracle manage to break up the rock, how does he intend to haul away the mountain of rubble using only a backhoe? And in half a day, no less.

The contractor is undaunted. He drives his trusty backhoe straight ahead, coming to a stop 20 feet away from the boulder. Then he starts to dig a hole.

The backhoe digs and digs. In a few hours it has hollowed out a pit 25 feet deep and 25 feet wide.

The contractor then drives around to the back of the boulder and carefully, foot by foot, shoves it to the edge and then over, into the hole. He finishes the job by pushing dirt into the pit and smoothing over the surface. Soon the road is flat and ready for repaving.

Then he goes to lunch.

Now think about it. The job the contractor took on seemed totally impossible to everyone in town, even the experts. No one believed it could be done. You probably didn't think it could be done, either. No one believed except the contractor. He saw what others didn't see; then he did what others couldn't do. Because he had vision, persistence, and passion, he did the seemingly impossible.

He knew that there's always a way.

"The block of granite which was an obstacle in the pathway of the weak, became a stepping-stone in the pathway of the strong."

—*Thomas Carlyle, English writer and philosopher*

Let's Sum Up

You can do it. Like the contractor could do it.

How? Let's review.

- **In times of crisis, view adversity as an opportunity rather than a loss.** Use every setback that comes your way as a wake-up call, a challenge, and a learning tool to help you reach your goals.

- **Try to see a way when others see a wall.** Think beyond the box, color outside the lines, leap while others are asleep. And remember—there is no box if you aren't in one.
- **Go ahead, take risks.** When you do nothing, nothing happens. Life only goes forward when you push it in that direction.
- **Always strive to keep a positive mindset.** Nothing is more important in business and in life than a positive attitude. It is the royal road to getting everything you wish for.
- **Avoid negativity.** It is a monster with a thousand tentacles. Each tentacle will pull you in and drag you down. Negativity sucks.
- **Use every tool in your get-it-done toolkit.** Use humor, tenacity, assertion, positivity, passion, energy, self-talk, visualizations, boldness, physical fitness, and the models set by others who've blazed the trail of achievement with vision and persistence.
- **Set goals for yourself; then pursue them with unbending intent.** Let each goal be a star in your eye and a sun on your horizon.
- **Step out to stand out.** Let the world know you're here, and don't be shy about it. Use whatever works. All selling is self-selling. Become your own brand.
- **Be passionate about everything you do.** Remember the hope and enthusiasm you had as a child. Rekindle it now. Passion is the fuel you burn to set the world on fire.
- **Stay fit.** Exercise. Cultivate right eating and sensible living habits. You'll see the difference in every aspect of your performance. The Greeks talked about "a sound mind in a sound body." Go for it.
- **Come at life and the competition with everything you've got.** Don't hold back. Marshal all your forces, gather all your strengths, then reach for the moon and pluck it out of the sky. If you miss, well, then you might end up grabbing a star instead.
- **Persist, persevere, and never give up.** When the going gets tough, the tough get going.
- **Be polite, be thoughtful, be helpful, and stand by your principles.** Treasure your virtues. When everything else falls away, these remain. Strive to develop character.

"Here's the secret, what I call the shortcut to creating your life the way you want it: *Be happy now*.

That's it. If you can be happy right now, in this moment, you will have achieved whatever you want. Why? Because underneath everything you say you want is the desire for happiness."

—Joe Vitale in The Attractor Factor

Going Proactive

A few years ago I was invited to make calls on a telethon for the Children's Miracle Network.

The network needed money in the worst way, they told me, and people weren't responding well to their fund drives. They knew I was a specialist at getting viewers to open their pockets, and they urged me to use all my selling skills to help them meet their financial goals.

On the day of the telethon I took my seat at a phone desk and then looked around. Seated nearby were dozens of high-profile celebrities from football, hockey, and show business. I felt pretty special. Then the show went on the air, the emcee started to do his sales pitch, and one by one the phones began to ring. The celebrities picked them up and dutifully took pledges.

Great. We were all here pulling for a common cause. Soon, however, I noticed that the phones weren't ringing all *that* often. I also saw that my fellow volunteers were basically sitting there waiting for the calls to come to them. A golden opportunity was being missed, I thought to myself. It was time to go proactive.

As luck would have it, I'd brought my address book with me that day. It contained a lengthy phone list of friends and people I did business with. I picked up the phone and started calling people on the list, asking them for a donation. After a few minutes of serious dialing and dialogue, several celebrities sitting nearby looked over at me and asked what I was doing. We're supposed to answer the phones, they insisted, not call out on them.

"Who says?" I replied. "Anything that works, right? And listen, if I had waited for the phone to ring all my life, I'd never be in business today." Then I called another friend.

By the end of the telethon I had raised over $20,000 for the children, far more than anyone else working the phones that day.

So figure it out. Don't break up the boulder. Instead, dig a hole and bury it. Look for the weak points, the loopholes, the opportunities. They're always there. See what others don't see. Go beyond the limits others put on you. Be daring; take chances. There's always a way.

"The truth of the matter is," Tony Robbins once remarked, "that there's *nothing* you can't accomplish if (1) you clearly decide what it is that you're absolutely committed to achieving, (2) you're willing to take massive action, (3) you notice what's working or not, and (4) you continue to change your approach until you achieve what you want, using whatever life gives you along the way."

Great advice.

"A wish changes nothing. A decision changes everything."

—*Me*

The Best Advice I Ever Received

When I was a boy, my father deserted our family and left my mother alone to support me, my brother, and my two sisters on a schoolteacher's salary. Where would she find the means and determination to carry off such an enormous task? There were four of us to feed, clothe, take care of. It seemed an impossible challenge.

But my mother never ran from responsibilities. She went straight ahead, never back. This was where I learned the importance of always moving ahead. Somehow, by working hard, going without, and making ends meet, she managed to get us all through the early years and raised us all to be decent, hardworking kids.

One day when I was a teenager I asked her how she was able to support all of us, work so hard for so little money, and still keep her cool. "What you have to do in life, Tony," she told me, "is believe in yourself, make your best efforts, and let the Good Lord do the rest."

The Good Lord—whatever you believe the Good Lord to be.

Listen, folks, life is always calling to you, asking you—begging you—to take advantage of the opportunities it brings to your door. All you have to do is recognize these opportunities, do your utmost to bring them to success, and then let the great wheels and gears of the universe spin as they will and take care of the rest.

Just as my mother said to do. And just as the great German poet Johann Wolfgang von Goethe advised 250 years ago in words that should be written in large letters on every living room wall and in every classroom in the United States.

"Begin it now," writes Goethe. "Until one is committed there is hesitancy, the chance to draw back, always ineffectiveness. Concerning all acts of initiative and creation, there is one elementary truth the ignorance of which kills countless ideas and splendid plans. That the moment you definitely commit yourself, *then providence moves too.* All sorts of things happen to help you that could never otherwise have occurred. A whole stream of events issues from the decision, raising in your favor all manner of unforeseen incidents and meetings and material assistance, which no man could have dreamed would have come his way. Whatever you can do or dream you can, begin it. Boldness has genius, power, and magic in it. Begin it now."

Begin it now. Hitch your wagon to a star. Be positive, be creative, be different, be fit, be fair, take risks, have vision, believe you can, give it everything you've got, never quit—and success in business and in life will come to you as surely as the sun rises in the morning and sets at night.

Meanwhile, I wish you great good fortune in reaching your goals and in this awesome adventure of living. You are standing at the beginning of a road that leads to wonderful things. Today is the first day of the rest of your life. Begin it now. And may great good fortune bless your way.

Because there always is—a way. And *you* can do it.

20

PS—Watch and Shop: The Inside Story

Politics, Crisis, and Coming Home Again

People often ask me how I got started on TV, and how I went about developing close relationships with major selling channels like HSN and QVC.

I've told you lots of stories already about my business origins. You know the tale of Bud Paxson and how, along with Phyllis Diller, he helped me become the first celebrity to sell product on a TV shopping channel. Since I hear this question so often, however, I thought I'd add a short PS chapter and answer it in a little greater depth.

When I first began with the Home Shopping Network, nobody at the channel seemed to quite know their position or place. Things were constantly up in the air, always in the process of morphing into something else. One day early on one of the execs from the network cornered me. Management, he announced in hushed tones, had made a command decision. I was *not* to hang out with any of the other show hosts on the channel.

This seemed like an odd request. What was behind it?

As it turned out, management was a jealous mistress. It didn't want other show hosts on the channel, many of whom were incredibly talented, to know that I was being groomed as a celebrity host to sell my own line of products. If they did they might say to themselves, "Hmmm! If Tony Little can do that, why can't I?" Mutiny and chaos would presumably follow.

In the early days, too, Roy Spears, the other brilliant half of HSN (along with Bud Paxson), helped me settle in at the network and was continuously supportive. So was Bob Scidmore, one of the big-time financial partners at the channel at the time, whose help I still appreciate today. Everything seemed fine between everyone until one day Roy Spears's son, who also worked for HSN, asked his father to *fire* me. Wow! Rumor had it that junior might be jealous. Or maybe he just didn't like me.

Giving me the boot, however, would not be so easy, considering that I was breaking every sales record, developing innovative selling concepts, and helping drive the amazingly rapid growth of this new network. Not wanting to kill the goose that laid the golden commercial, I suppose, Roy held his ground against his son's pestering and kept me on. I remember his loyalty.

At any rate, it was not until the network became more established and its systems and management teams more in place that things loosened up, we were allowed to socialize freely with one another, and petty jealousies were brushed under the rug. These were my first tastes of network politics. They would also *not* be the last.

I did my thing at HSN for 10 years, selling, selling, selling, and in the process learning the ins and outs of this amazing company. During this time there was a constant change of presidents and regimes, all of which I somehow managed to survive. These revolving-door network heads were, by and large, all solid administrators who knew the business, and who didn't think it necessary to constantly reinvent the wheel. If it works, let it keep working.

Then a new president with the last name of Dyer took control.

In my opinion this man of intelligence but limited vision clearly did not understand either the mechanics or the psychology of home shopping. From the moment he took command at HSN he instituted a series of changes that in many people's opinions made no sense, and that created pandemonium up and down the network's chain of command. When I saw that these new policies were gumming up the works, and worse, when I realized that my own selling strategies were being questioned, I felt something had to give.

Let me point out that during this 10-year period, besides being aligned with HSN, I was selling steadily in Canada on the Shopping Channel. (I was actually the first celebrity host to sell on TV in this country,) I debuted there in 1987, and over eight years developed a solid friendship with everyone at the station. I was also deep into infomercial sales at the time, along with the very successful retailing of my product brands. In other words, I was financially sound and in a safe position to make changes.

After a lot of agonizing—I had, after all, grown up on the Home Shopping Network—I decided to leave HSN and move on.

That next year I moved on to England. There I sold live on the English QVC network, and over the next year churned out such huge numbers that Doug Briggs, president of QVC TV, called and said he wanted to talk. I first met Doug when I started selling for QVC in the States. Now, seeing that I was continuing to put up the big numbers, he had a proposition to make me that would be hard to pass up.

QVC, he said, would give me 50 percent ownership of Q-Fit, a new start-up, in-house company that QVC was about to launch. I would build my brand and sell fitness products for QVC *in-house*. I would no longer be an independent salesman, but a permanent employee of this gigantic company, with a permanent monetary share. I had already sold multimillions of dollars' worth of my own product on HSN, and had as well reached outside of the network to capture 81 countries of distribution. These were larger sales figures than any salesman in TV sales had ever logged (or ever would as of this writing). Now QVC wanted me to do the same thing for them in a *proprietary* way, selling their products exclusively in-house. It was a deal that was right up my alley, Doug Briggs assured me.

Or so we all thought.

For as great a man as Doug was, he simply could not contend with the politics that exploded the moment I took the helm at Q-Fit. From the get-go executives were brought in from retail companies who didn't understand the way I worked. They wanted to give me ground-up instruction in salesmanship technique, and worse, wanted to tell me *what* to sell. It became more and more difficult to develop product concepts into brand with this red tape and meddling. A mess!

In retrospect, it probably would have been better for everyone if QVC had simply left me as an outside independent company. At any rate, it wasn't to be. Within 10 months I resigned and went to work full-time for QVC in the United Kingdom, where I'd sold product on and off for more than a decade. I stayed on with this English station, avoiding the American TV market for more than a year.

Then an amazing thing happened. Mr. Dyer miraculously disappeared as president of the Home Shopping Network, and a new regime replaced him.

Yeah, baby!

Right away I contacted the VP of the Home Shopping Network, Jeff Tarashi, who put me in touch with the new president, Mark Bozak. Together we sat down and discussed the prospect of my coming home to my first love, HSN. Jeff helped paved the way for my return, and soon I was back in the saddle, doing my selling thing.

Success was immediate, and the network was my home again. We were all making lots of money. I loved the way HSN's entrepreneurial spirit prevailed. I loved the show hosts. I loved how the HSN staff cared so deeply about the integrity of my products. I loved the teamwork and the support I got from buyers, operators, and the customer service people. All of them really cared about providing great service and products to HSN's vast consumer base.

Today HSN is under a new management team brought in by the famous TV mogul (and creator of Fox Broadcasting) Barry Diller. Diller signed a new CEO to HSN, Mindy Grossman, a former global president of Nike.

The moment Mindy and I met I fell in love with her heart for the business, with her management style, and with the care she showed to her employees. Mindy was not afraid to make decisions, right or wrong. This is one of the chief signs, I believe, of a great CEO. I was one of her earliest supporters.

Today she's still there leading the successful charge at HSN.

In all, I finally feel that I've come home to HSN for good. You can never predict when a new management team will be brought into any company, of course, or when policies will suddenly shift. As long as the network avoids messing with what works, however, and as long as they don't try to fix what isn't broken, I'm a happy camper. The company and its people, I believe, will always prosper. Because there's always a way—especially when you believe in yourself and have a company that believes in *you*.

Getting Started in Infomercials

It was 1992 and infomercials were just becoming popular on American TV. Just as I had wanted my own TV show in the 1980s, now I had a jones for producing an infomercial. I felt the fit would be perfect.

A gentleman named Earl Greenburg, a former VP of NBC and a graduate of Wharton School of Business, had recently taken over at HSN as president of a new division called HSN Direct (as in direct TV selling). Earl saw me at work on one of my videos and called the president, Jim Lawless, to ask about me. Jim told him I was "the complete selling machine."

Earl then contacted me and asked if I'd like to learn the ins and outs of infomercial production from him. I said I absolutely would.

The deal was that Earl would train me for free and I'd help him improve his workout skills for free. Unlike a lot of unmotivated young people these days who think they should be CEO of a company in the first two weeks, and who don't want to do *anything* without getting paid, I knew that in both business and life you always have to give something to get something back.

It turned out that Earl was a great mentor and he quickly taught me the ropes of infomercial selling. I really valued our relationship and we've remained great friends through the years.

One day Earl called and *ordered* me to go directly to Las Vegas and attend the Second Annual Infomercial Awards Dinner. He was going to be the master of ceremonies that night, he told me, and would make very sure I got seated at a good table.

And boy did I get a seat! Earl sat me at this huge round table in front of the stage surrounded on the left and right by infomercial big shots like Bill Guthy and Greg Renker of Guthy-Renker's celebrity-sponsored television products; Kevin Harrington from National Media, a big infomercial company; and Mike Levy, one of the most entertaining personalities on TV and the host of *Amazing Discoveries*, a very hot infomercial format show of the 1990s.

As it turned out, Earl had another engagement that evening and had to leave the dinner early. As he rose from the table he turned and addressed everyone there.

"This is Tony Little," he announced, putting his hand on my shoulder. "Whoever leaves here tonight and signs this young man is going to make millions!"

Game on. Earl was so respected in the business that everyone's ears went up like antennas when he said this and I suddenly became the center of attention. Before the night was through I'd made a deal with National Media. They were an international company, and I didn't much care what language the customers spoke. If someone out there in Viewerville had a big gut or a big butt, they needed my help.

I also landed my first fitness show with *Amazing Discoveries*, where, 81 countries later, I *became* an amazing discovery myself.

That's basically how I got started in the infomercial field.

I shot my first infomercial, called "Target Training," in 1993 for the company called National Media. John Turchi, one of the execs, was wary of the deal and called George Simone, a friend of mine and the manager at the time for Connie Stevens and (if memory serves me correctly) Sophia Loren.

Turchi said to George, "Hey, I've just blown a quarter of a million dollars on this blond ponytailed weight lifter yelling it up on TV. Am I nuts?"

George said not to worry, that Turchi now had "an 800-pound gorilla in selling on your team. Just wait and see."

As it turned out, the three videos in the Target Training series went on to sell over seven million copies for a profit of more than $100 million.

A few weeks after the first show was aired and the profits were rolling in, I got a call from John Turchi from his car cell phone (a startling new piece of technology at the time). He informed me that I'd broken all previous records for selling on infomercials, and that he was glad he'd taken the risk. You can do it!

Some months later, after sales calmed down, I then sold the retail rights to Target Training—how I kept these I don't know, but I did—to a medium-sized company called PPI in New Jersey.

A few months after the sale I went to dinner with the president of PPI, Donald Kasen. He was a terrific guy and we had a sparkling conversation that night. When we finished our meal and got to the dessert (which I didn't eat), Donald reached into his pocket and took out a folded bank check with great ceremony—the real dessert. It was the first I'd received for selling a product in retail stores for four months. I unfolded it and read.

It was for $1.2 million.

"Hey," I shouted at the top of my lungs, as everyone in the restaurant turned and looked. "I really *love* this business!!!"

Do you know why shopping channels are so successful around the world? It's simple. Home shopping has time on its side. It has the luxury to slowly and painstakingly educate consumers in the exact features and benefits of each product, and to show how these features fit into viewer's lives. Retail stores are not so blessed. They have too many products on their shelves, and too little time to explain how each product works. This is one reason why home shopping, and the infomercial in particular, is one of the greatest selling tools ever invented.